SCOTLAND, MULTINATIONALS AND THE THIRD WORLD

SCOTLAND, MULTINATIONALS AND THE THIRD WORLD

edited by Stephen Maxwell

MAINSTREAM
PUBLISHING

in conjunction with
Scottish Education and Action for Development
Edinburgh 1982

ACKNOWLEDGEMENTS

The idea of a volume of essays exploring the triangular relationship between Scotland, multinationals and the Third World was conceived by Mark Lazarowicz in his time as an Organiser of Scottish Education and Action for Development. Thanks are due in addition to Joyce Macmillan and Anne Chisholm for their help in typing and editing and to the authors for their patience during the long gap between surrendering their manuscripts and the appearance of this volume.

Cover design by Deborah Harvey.

This book is published by
MAINSTREAM PUBLISHING COMPANY
(EDINBURGH) LTD.
25a South West Thistle Street Lane,
Edinburgh EH2 1EW.

ISBN 0 906391 28 8

Printed in Great Britain
by Spectrum Printing Company, Edinburgh.

CONTENTS

INTRODUCTION

Scotland offers a good vantage point from which to examine the changing role of multinational companies in the world economy. In two centuries she has evolved from being a seed-bed of multinational companies to being a satellite of multinational empires based elsewhere.

Stephen Maxwell's essay in this volume traces the course of that evolution. In the eighteenth century the expansion was to the West in the form of companies trading in the slave-produced commodities of tobacco, sugar and cotton. In the nineteenth, the expansion was to the East through companies with interests in manufacturing, agency management and plantation agriculture as well as trading.

While Scotland's overseas expansion depended absolutely on her status as a junior partner of the British Empire, Scottish entrepreneurs were not content merely to ride on the coat tails of English enterprise. As the Scottish challenge to the monopoly of the East India Company demonstrated in the early nineteenth century, the Scottish expansion had its own leadership, as well as its own backward lines of communication to the Scottish economy.

It the Empire gave the Scottish economy its opportunity, it also hastened its decline. The profits generated by the overseas expansion were as likely to be transformed into portfolio investment in North America and the Dominions as invested in Scottish industry. And within Britain, economic and cultural centralisation around the Imperial capital eroded Scotland's capacity to respond to the decline of the Imperial economy. Like a Third World country she became dependent for much of her economic development and innovation on foreign capital.

The subject of Roger Jeffery's essay—the firm of James Finlay of Glasgow—is atypical of Scottish multinationals with eighteenth century origins by virtue of its survival to the present day. Taking up the current company Chairman's description of the firm as "merchant adventurers", Jeffery argues that the firm's history in the nineteenth century makes it a poor example of that 'merchant capital' which in the view of some analysts carries a particularly heavy responsibility for the 'underdevelopment' of Third World economies. Starting life in the eighteenth-century sugar and cotton trade, Finlay's had built up a capital base in textile manufacturing in Scotland by the end of the century before embarking on an overseas expansion, first in the rice, silk and tea trades in India and China and then in textile manufacture and tea cultivation in India. The restructuring which the company has undertaken since the 1960's, closing down its surviving Scottish textile mills and reducing its plantation interests in the Third World

7

while expanding into merchant banking, offshore services and confectionery in the United Kingdom, has perhaps brought it closer to the model of merchant capital than it ever came in the nineteenth century.

The Glasgow-based textile firm of Coats Patons represents a younger generation of multinational companies based on manufacturing rather than trading. Its first overseas venture was in the United States, where it opened a mill in 1865. Major expansion in the Third World did not come until after the Second World War when the company established factories in Latin America and Asia while running down its Scottish labour force.

Alan Sinclair explores the part which Coats Patons' Indian affiliate Madura Coats plays in the company's international strategy. His inquiry confirms the competitive advantages which a multinational company derives from its capacity to switch investment internationally in response to differences in labour costs or changes in market access, its ability to "source" orders for its different production points and its use of transfer pricing to minimise its tax liability. And it provides an individual insight into the ways in which the Third World management of a multinational company can squeeze extra profits for its shareholders by sacrificing the health and safety of its local workers and exploiting the venality of local trade unions.

The emergence in the twentieth century of the multinational company as a dominant fact—some would say *the* dominant fact—of the modern economy is traced in Alan Sinclair's second essay. One estimate is that 50% of the total trade of the non-Communist nations is attributable to multinational companies. Today British-owned multinationals produce twice as much abroad as they export from the United Kingdom. The importance of multinational companies to the Scottish economy is summed up in the fact that non-United Kingdom multinationals contributed 54% of the total of new manufacturing jobs in Scotland between 1954 and 1974 and no less than 74% between 1969-1974. There is no factor in domestic or international economic activity—trade, prices, investment, employment, monetary policy, technological development—which is not critically influenced by the activities of the multinational companies. Sinclair's claim that the multinationals are the planners and shapers of modern society is well-attested.

John Firn's contributions focus on a question of great practical importance at a time when the flow of United States' investment to Scotland has abated since the flood-tide of the 1960's. How far is Scotland now in competition with the Third World as a location for new multinational investment? He argues that the growing technological content and capital intensity of industry and its consequences for a highly skilled labour force, mean that competition is more likely to come from other peripheral developed economies than from the Third World. Competition from goods produced by multinational companies in Third World countries, including

8

indigenous multinationals—a category which has only recently begun to attract academic attention—offers a serious threat in a limited number of sectors, notably electrical consumer goods, textiles, shipbuilding and steel. However Firn reminds us that imports from Third World countries command only a fraction of the overall market for manufactured goods in developed countries, barely 3% in the United Kingdom in 1980. And he argues strongly against a protectionist response, recommending instead a strategy of positive adaptation including direct investment by Scottish firms in the Third World individually and through joint ventures with Third World companies.

One of the acknowledged causes of the weakness of developing countries in the face of multinational companies is the absence of strong trade unions. But in the developed countries where relatively strong trade unions do exist how effective has their response to the multinational challenge been?

Nigel Howarth begins his assessment by clearing away what remains of the assumption that the internationalisation of capital will automatically call forth its antithesis in the shape of a united international trade union movement. Rather, an effective trade union response requires to be painstakingly constructed through reform of existing trade union institutions and attitudes. He urges a strengthening of international trade union contacts and the extension of trade union information and education services with particular emphasis on the Third World dimension of the activities of multinational companies. Above all the labour movement must break with its traditionally 'reactive' role to take the offensive through national and international labour combines within multinational companies, and the development of 'alternative planning' as practised by the Lucas Aerospace Combine.

In his discussion of dependent industrialisation Rhys Jenkins takes up one of the key controversies in the debate on the role of multinational companies in development. Can a process of industrialisation which is dependent on foreign firms, or on production for export, contribute to the development of an independent economic base for Third World countries? In Jenkins' view the post-war record suggests not. The strategy of building Third World industries through import substitution has led to an intensification of foreign control through the growth of manufacturing subsidiaries of multinational companies, increased outflow of dividends, royalties and interest payments. Meanwhile the strategy of export-led growth has added to the Third World's traditional role as a supplier of raw materials to the developed world a new role as a supplier of cheap labour.

Jenkins warns against the view of some radical Third World lobbyists that capitalist industrialisation in the Third World does not qualify as development simply because it is exploitative. By such a standard Britain's own industrial revolution in the nineteenth century would not qualify as development. Nevertheless the dominance of the multinational company in Third World industrialisation does alter the weight of the factors in the development equation. Where the surplus accumulated by capitalist exploitation is externally controlled it is the less likely to be reinvested in the economy which produced it.

Stephen Young and Neil Hood tell the story of one of Scotland's most bruising encounters with multinational companies.

In 1967 the United States' automobile company Chrysler bought out the ailing British company Rootes including its plant at Linwood opened four years earlier to grandiose claims of the rebirth of a Scottish car industry. Due to a combination of inadequate investment in new models, poor labour relations, the deteriorating financial position of the American parent and the onset of the oil crisis in 1973, Chrysler's United Kingdom operations failed to achieve viability. In 1975, in a demonstration of what the authors call "multinational imperialism pure and simple", Chrysler held a pistol to the Government's head—pay up or we close down.Facing an upsurge of Scottish Nationalism the Government pledged a maximum of £126m. to save the United Kingdom operation with its 9500 Linwood jobs. But in 1978 in another demonstration of multinational imperialism, Chrysler sold its entire European operations to the French firm Peugeot-Citroen, without consulting the Government. Three years later the remaining 4700 workers at Linwood voted 2-1, against their shop stewards' advice, to accept the final closure of the plant by Peugeot.

The episode provides confirmation, if that were needed, of the bargaining power and lack of accountability of multinational companies even in developed countries. But the authors also point to critical weaknesses in the Government's response. Intellectually, the Government failed to appreciate the degree of international integration in the car industry, specifically the need for Chrysler's Scottish operation to be fully integrated into the company's European strategy. And politically the Government failed to make the most of what bargaining power it possessed.

Scotland has been familiar with the operations of manufacturing multinationals since the advent of the Singer sewing-machine company in 1858. Her first encounter with the resource-based multinationals familiar to so many Third World countries came only with the discovery of oil reserves off the Scottish coast.

George Rosie deploys his skills as an investigative journalist to unravel the complex commercial manoeuvres which the oil discoveries stimulated around the Cromarty Firth. It is a story of free-wheeling, buccaneering entrepreneurship which in 1982 seems already to belong to a distant age of Scottish politics and economic development.

Introduction

The value of Rosie's account lies in the vivid insight it provides into the essentially speculative and opportunistic character of many multinational initiatives and into the way in which multinational companies seek the help of local allies in navigating political and legal shoals. It incidentally explodes the notion that multinational companies are omnipotent and omniscient. The chief financial gainers from the Cromarty Firth initiatives were not the multinationals but some local farmers and businessmen. The social and environmental cost, in Shetland and elsewhere around Scotland's coasts, is only now being counted as the high-tide of oil-related development recedes.

Scotland's own experience in the last two decades illustrates some of the problems of basing a development strategy on multinational investment. It is hardly fair to attribute the increase in Scottish unemployment from 90,000 at the beginning of the 1960's to over 300,000 in the early 1980's to the priority given by successive Governments in that period to attracting foreign investment. But from the perspective of 1982 it appears that jobs brought to Scotland by foreign investment may have been purchased at too high a price, not so much in money terms as in terms of the accelerated erosion of the already weak social and institutional foundations of the Scottish economy. In a decade in which new multinational investment threatens to be more elusive, with Scotland facing stronger competition if not from Third World countries then from other European nations, fashionable wisdom has rediscovered the attractions of nurturing native enterprise in the hope that from little acorns great oaks may grow. The switch of emphasis—conversion would be too strong a word—may have come too late. Following two decades of positive discrimination by the state in favour of foreign capital, the economic recession may have injured the once vital native sector of the Scottish economy beyond the hope of recovery. Scottish opinion may yet have to acknowledge that the challenge of Scottish development is of Third World dimensions.

Stephen Maxwell

SCOTLAND'S COMMERCIAL EMPIRE: AN HISTORICAL PERSPECTIVE ON SCOTLAND'S RELATIONS WITH THE THIRD WORLD

by Stephen Maxwell

Scotland first came into sustained contact with countries which today form part of the Third World through shared membership of the British Empire. In the eighteenth century and the first half of the nineteenth century most Scots regarded the Empire, unblinkingly, as a provider of career opportunities, a source of commercial profit or simply as empty space awaiting colonisation. Then in the mid-nineteenth century David Livingstone's African exploits cast a pall of religiosity over British imperial ambitions.

The loss of Empire in the twentieth century reinforced the sentimentalist view. As the reality of Empire retreated before the myth the commercial urge behind Scotland's participation was forgotten. Even the emergence in the 1970's of a new political militancy in the Third World did little to modify British perceptions. Compared to an Empire which survives in the popular imagination as a kaleidoscope of heroic images—Livingstone on the Zambesi, Highlanders storming to the Relief of Lucknow, Aberdeen clippers racing the wind homewards from the East—the Third World cannot but seem remote and problematic, a table of statistics or a subject of moralising speeches.

Scotland played little part in the earliest and cruellest form of British exploitation of the Third World—the slave trade between Africa and the Americans in the seventeenth and eighteenth centuries. Her economic backwardness and the poor access Scottish merchants had to royal patronage after the Union of the Crowns in 1603 meant that no Scottish Company was in a postion to challenge the Chartered privileges of the English Royal Africa Company established in 1672.[1] In any case in a mercantilist age the absence of Scottish colonies in the West Indies or America would have left a Scottish trading company without any guaranteed outlets.

Scotland was nevertheless a major beneficiary of the slave trade. Even before the Parliamentary Union of 1707 gave Scotland official access to the English colonies, Scottish merchants had developed a substantial contraband trade with England's West Indian and American possessions in defiance of the English Navigation Laws which sought to preserve the trade for English ships. And after the Union the largely slave-produced colonial commodities of tobacco, sugar and cotton played an important role in Scotland's economic development.

Glasgow was geographically well placed for the trade with the tobacco colonies of Virginia and Maryland, especially in time of war when the route around Northern Ireland provided the safest line of communication. In the mid-century tobacco boom Glasgow merchants were importing as much tobacco as London and all the other British ports together. In the early 1770's the tobacco trade accounted for 80% of all Scottish imports.

There is dispute among economic historians about the importance of the tobacco trade to Scotland's economic growth in the eighteenth century. The trade certainly afforded an outlet for Scottish cloth, leather goods, plantation equipment, guns and other manufactures, but for the Scottish economy as a whole the colonial markets were insignificant compared to the British market. While some tobacco merchants were partners in early ventures into factory production they do not seem to have been major providers of industrial capital, preferring to invest their profits in land, property, securities or banking stock.

The Glasgow tobacco merchants had always been general merchants ready to trade in whatever commodity promised a handsome return. Even before the American War of Independence many of them had interests in the West Indian trade in sugar, rum and cotton. The breach in the British trading monopoly with North America caused by American independence encouraged them to diversify further into the West Indian trade.

The cultivation of West Indian cane sugar as of other West Indian crops under the plantation system was more dependent on slave labour than tobacco grown in America where the pattern of small-scale settler cultivation was only gradually replaced by the plantation system.

The sugar trade provided an important source of employment and wealth in Greenock and Port Glasgow from the eighteenth century through to the twentieth. In addition to merchandising, it supported extensive shipping activities and in the nineteenth century a large sugar refining industry. The peak years came after the reduction of the duty on raw colonial sugar in the 1840's when no fewer than fifteen sugar refineries were operating in Greenock. By the 1880's however competition from subsidised sugar beet from the European continent had begun to erode Greenock's pre-eminence. The decline was accelerated by the decision in 1881 of the town's leading refiner, Lyle's, to build a major new factory in London in preference to Greenock.[2]

The slave-produced commodity of greatest importance to Scotland's industrial development was, of course, cotton. Imports of raw cotton to the Clyde jumped from 0.15 million lbs. per annum in 1770-74 to 7.5 million lbs in 1800 and this was only part of Scotland's cotton imports as much of Scottish industry was dependent on fine yarn spun south of the Border.[3] According to one contemporary estimate in 1820 Scotland's cotton manufacture supplied over 50% of Scotland's total manufacturing employment. And as a catalyst of industrial and technological change the importance of cotton was beyond statistical measurement.

In the eighteenth century Scottish companies had been largely excluded from the most profitable field of overseas commercial enterprise by the East India Company's monopoly of British trade with India and China. However individual Scots were by no means excluded from a share in the rewards of Britain's Indian possession. Many gained positions in the Company's prolific bureaucracy. When Henry Dundas, Scotland's political manager between 1775 and 1801, was a member of the Company's Board of Control he made such generous use of his power of patronage that Walter Scott was moved to describe the Company as "the corn chest of Scotland where we poor gentry must send our youngest sons as we send black cattle to the south". But some of Scotland's human exports to India survived, to return eventually as rich 'Nabobs' whose social pretensions and political ambitions John Galt satirised in his novel "The Member".

While defending its monopoly of trade between Britain and the East, the East India Company allowed private merchants to carry on trade and business within India. Here again Scottish merchants were prominent, particularly in the distinctive role of commission agents in the late eighteenth and nineteenth centuries. Business houses with names such as Fairlie, Ferguson, Gilmore, Andrew Yule, Smith Mackenzie, Findlay Duff, Burns McVicar, Ritchie Stewart and Company testify to Scottish commercial vigour.

The Calcutta based houses were particularly active in the manufacture of indigo in the opening decades of the nineteenth century. At the height of the indigo boom in 1828 they controlled three hundred indigo factories employing half a million Indian families with an annual output worth up to £3m. more than the £1¼m. it cost to maintain them. One consortium, Richards Mackintosh Yrissair Matheson, Fletcher Alexander and Company is reported to have owned fifty-six factories which before the collapse of the indigo trade between 1829-33 represented capital assets of £2m.[4].

Scots merchants like Kirkman Finlay, the chief architect of the firm of James Finlay of Glasgow and James Matheson, co-founder of the China firm of Jardine Matheson, took the lead in challenging the East India Company's monopoly of the Eastern trade.

The origins of the Finlay fortune lay in the eigthteenth century sugar and cotton trade with the West Indies. Kirkman's father was a West Indian merchant who diversified from cotton trading to cotton manufacture. When the East India Company's monopoly on the Indian trade was finally raised in 1813, Finlay's, by then under Kirkman's leadership, developed wide trading interests with India to add to their Scottish textile interests. When the East India monopoly on the China trade was ended in 1833 the firm was again quick to seize the new opportunities.

Finlay's Indian interests were consolidated in 1870 by the establishment of a jute mill in Calcutta and by the expansion of its trading interest in silk, rice and cotton. By the end of the century Finlay's had begun the move into tea that was to make it by 1939 the largest firm in the Indian tea industry and the owner of 20,000 acres of tea plantations in Kenya. At the beginning of the Second World War Finlay's Calcutta office had 140,000 employees on its books.[5]

Asia was a major field for Scottish commercial enterprise in the nineteenth century. In 1818 a Dumfries-born surgeon William Jardine, left the East India Company after sixteen years' service. By skilful use of the 'privilege' tonnage allowed him as an East India Officer, he had acquired sufficient capital to start trading on his own account. In 1832 he joined a Sutherland man James Matheson, who had developed an agency in the 'country' trade between China and India, to create the firm of Jardine Matheson. When the East India monopoly was raised in 1833 Jardine Matheson sent the first 'free' cargo of tea to Britain. The firm was to prove one of the most successful of the East India Company's successors: its 'Pickwick' tea mixture captured a major part of the old Company's market.

Jardine Matheson was one of the leading traders in opium between the Indian border states and China, a trade carried on in defiance of the edict of the Chinese Emperor. When in 1839 the Chinese Government finally took action against the European traders, restricting their movements and impounding their opium stocks, William Jardine, by then the leading Canton merchant, travelled to London as head of a delegation of China merchants to persuade Lord Palmerston of the need for British military intervention. The Treaty of Nanking which brought the Opium War to an end in 1842 ceded Hong Kong to Britain, and from that base Jardine Matheson vigorously exploited the new commercial freedoms guaranteed under the Treaty. The firm took a leading part in developing Shanghai, opened up 1,350 miles of the Yangtse to Western trade, launched China's first steamship, published her first newspaper and built her first railway. By the turn of the century it employed 113,000 people throughout Asia.[6]

A key company in the history of British India was the British Indian Steam Navigation Company founded by William Mackinnon. Mackinnon was founding partner in 1847 of the firm of Mackenzie, Mackinnon and Company, merchants, of Calcutta. In 1856 he extended his interests into shipping with the formation of the Calcutta and Burmah Steam Navigation Company. One of the firm's first contracts was the transport of British troops to India to suppress the Mutiny of 1857.[7]

The Calcutta and Burmah Company was absorbed into the British Indian

Steam Navigation Company in 1862. Engaged initially in the Asian trade, it extended its operations in 1871 to Zanzibar and the East Coast of Africa, a region which came to exercise a strong hold on Mackinnon's imagination. By the time of Mackinnon's death in 1893 the British Indian Company was operating a fleet of fifty-eight ships and employing 1,000 officers and 10,000 seamen.

The British India Company was one of a network of Scottish led or Scottish founded shipping concerns which helped to bind the Empire together. Prominent among them was 'Paddy' Henderson's of Glasgow. Originally ship insurance brokers, from 1841 the firm took a leading role in the extensive charter trade developed from Glasgow by shipowners like Hogarth, Burrell, Dunlop and Gardiner. The firm founded the Albion Line which pioneered the New Zealand and Eastern services before being amalgamated with its leading rival Shaw Savill in 1882. Henderson's was also involved in the formation of the British and Burmah steam Navigation Company in 1893.[8]

In 1869 Glasgow interests engaged in the palm-oil trade with West Africa helped to found the British and African Steam Navigation Company which later formed the basis of Alfred Jones' Liverpool based Elder Dempster Line. The Clan Line formed in 1878 in Liverpool by the firm of Cayzer Irvine for the Indian service, developed an important African trade with Glasgow in the closing decades of the century.

The 'Diamond K' Line was built up by John Kerr and Abram Lyle of Greenock between 1850 and 1870 to serve the West Indian trade. After Kerr's death in 1873, Lyle built the Cape Line into a major force on the Asian and African routes.[9]

The Peninsular and Oriental Line was founded by the Orcadian Arthur Anderson in 1839 with the support of mail contracts for Gibraltar and Alexandria. Although its headquarters were in London, in the latter part of the century half of its fleet was based in Greenock. Also in 1839 Glasgow interests combined with American and Liverpool firms to form the Cunard Company.

Mackinnon's outstanding successor in the Indian firm of Mackinnon, Mackenzie and Co. was James Lyle Mackay, later Lord Inchape. When in 1893 Mackay returned to Britain to take charge of the British India Company following Mackinnon's death his field of enterprise, in the words of the Dictionary of National Biography, "embraced the jute, tea and coal industries of Bengal, the cotton and wool industries of Madras, the seaborne trade between India and Burma, the Persian Gulf and East Africa, and many ancillary companies in the hinterland of these areas." But Mackay's supreme business achievement was the fusion between 1914 and 1920 of the British India Company with the P. and O. and other smaller lines to form a single group with a tonnage of two million under the P. and O. flag.[10]

Another transport giant of the Empire was the Irrawaddy Flotilla Company, founded in Rangoon, Burma, in 1865 on the initiative of Todd Findlay and Company with Henderson's as manager and major shareholder and with participation by Denny's of Dumbarton, shipbuilders, Clarks of Paisley, threadmakers, and other Scottish businesses. The firm rapidly developed a network of trading and commercial interests in Burma and beyond based on its dominance of the Irrawaddy Delta transport system. When the Bombay Burmah Trading Corporation entered into a dispute with King Thebaw of Upper Burma over timber dues, the British ultimatum which led to the Pagoda War of 1885 was delivered by an officer of the Irrawaddy Flotilla Company. On Thebaw's rejection of the ultimatum, the 10,000 strong Burma Field Force, which had been shipped from Madras by the British India Company, was carried up-river by the Flotilla Company's Fleet from Rangoon to Thebaw's capital of Mandalay to complete the annexation of Upper Burma.[11]

The Company continued to expand its operations until by the end of the 1920's it was operating 620 vessels carrying nine million passengers and one and one-quarter million tons of cargo each year, making it the "greatest inland water transport enterprise the world has ever known", according to a recent history of the Company.[12]

Henderson's was also the leading actor in a less successful inland shipping venture in South America. In 1886 the firm bought the ailing La Platense River Company on the River Plate in the Argentine and in two years, using some of the expertise they had acquired on the Irrawaddy, built it up to a strength of fifty vessels. But in the midst of Argentine's political crises this new venture never showed any real promise of achieving profitablity and it was wound up in 1890.

One of the most important nineteenth century Scottish industries dependent on a Third World commodity was the Dundee Jute industry. Dundee textile firms first turned to Indian jute when the Crimean War threatened their supplies of Russian flax. In its boom years between the 1850's and 1880's the Dundee textile industry, using both flax and jute, employed up to 30,000 people. In the 1860's some of the larger Dundee firms established baling plants in Bengal, the main source of the jute, as part of a strategy to replace transshipment via London with direct importation to Dundee.

But as early as 1855 there were signs that Dundee was not to be given a clear run. In that year the first jute mill in Bengal was opened under a Scots manager and with the help of Dundee mechanics and overseers. In 1857 the

Borneo Company, registered in London but with strong Scottish connections, opened the first power-loom factory in Bengal. Further expansion in India was encouraged by the high profits earned by these early mills. In 1870 the Glasgow based firm of James Finlay, already well established in a range of Indian operations, entered the jute industry. By 1875 the Samnuggar and Titaghur Company, floated in 1873 by a Scots consortium with participation by Dundee interests, was directly attacking the Dundee industry's markets in California and Australia. From the 1880's higher continental tariffs on jute imports increased the pressure on Dundee, and between 1882 and 1885 four new mills were opened in Calcutta. Although one of these mills was Dundee owned, in 1885 only 10% of the Indian industry as a whole was controlled from Dundee. The lead seems to have been taken by London and Glasgow interests in conjunction with 'overseas' firms like James Finlay and the Borneo Company or by Indian entrepreneurs, with Dundee technical expertise and managerial skills being brought in to reinforce the challenge to the home industry.[13]

One of the most successful Scottish firms with its beginning in Asia was the Burmah Petroleum Company. The Company was founded in 1871 as the Rangoon Oil Company and incorporated in Scotland as the Burmah Petroleum Company by David Sime Cargill in 1886. Its Burmese oil operations were modest but secure. In 1905 Burmah went to the rescue of the D'Arcy Oil Expoloration Company which was facing bankruptcy after several years of fruitless exploration in the Middle East. Three years later D'Arcy struck oil in the Zagros mountains in Iran. A new company, the Anglo-Persian, was floated to exploit the discoveries with Burmah putting up virtually all the capital. The issue of shares in Glasgow created an outburst of 'speculator's fever' with excited crowds queuing to purchase stock in the new company. Anglo-Persian was wholly owned by Burmah until in 1914 the British Government acquired a majority share and laid the foundations of British Petroleum.

Burmah had meanwhile continued to expand its trading interests in Asia and to develop its Burmese oil operations. It proved a profitable concern. Between 1928 and 1938 its ordinary stock yielded a handsome 22%. In 1946, in the post-war recovery boom, Burma had a largely Burmese labour force of 23,000. Its output of Burmese oil at less than 1% of world output represented 21% of Empire production at the time.

The Bombay Burmah Trading Company whose dispute with King Thebaw in 1885 had been the occasion if not the cause of the British annexation of Upper Burma, was another major Burmese firm of Scottish origin. The company was founded in 1863 under joint British and Indian ownership by William Wallace. Wallace, from Edinburgh, had worked in India as a merchant and agent since 1847 developing trading interests in many parts of Asia. In 1880 the company obtained concessions from King

18

Thebaw to exploit the teak forests of Upper Burma. The dispute which led to the British annexation in 1885 was occasioned by Thebaw's allegation that the Company had defrauded him of £70,000 of timber dues and its Burmese workers of £30,000 of wages. But behind were British fears of French encroachment on their commercial privileges and political influence and the lure of an overland trade route to China through Yunnan.[14]

In the Burmese teak trade the Bombay Burmah Trading Company was in competition with firms like Macgregor and Company and Steel and Company. When it extended its timber operations to Siam in 1890 it came into competition with yet another firm of Scottish provenance.

The Borneo Company was established with the encouragement of James Brooke, Rajah of Sarawak, by the firms of Paterson and Co. and MacEwan and Co. to develop Borneo's reserves of antimony and gold. But from headquarters in Singapore it came to control extensive trading and transport operations throughout the East, including a jute factory and a sugar refinery in India, dock interests in Singapore itself, rubber and gold in Sarawak, timber in Burma and Siam, and tea in Sumatra.[15]

Although Asia was the main field of Scottish commercial enterprise in the nineteenth century noon of Empire, the reputation of David Livingstone and the activities of the Scottish Church Missions ensured that the Dark Continent loomed large in the Scottish imagination. Indeed the dilution of commercial motives by religious and philanthropic sentiment helps to explain the poor economic record of some of the Scottish commercial ventures in Africa.

The Africa Lakes' Trading Company was formed in 1878 by a group of Glasgow businessmen associated with the Free Church to apply Livingstone's teaching that commerce and Christianity together would bring civilisation to Africa. Under the leadership of John and Frederick Moir the Company set out to persuade the African tribes around Lake Nyasa to develop conventional commerce to replace the commerce in slaves.

The Company failed in its aim of establishing a cash crop economy and remained commercially dependent on the traditional ivory trade. As a result its finances were never equal to the administrative and political responsibilities it had to assume in a region which was exposed to the Arab slave trade and which was increasingly the target of German and Portuguese imperial ambitions.

In 1891 following a quite unrealistic bid for Chartered status, the Company was relieved of its responsibilities and its territory put under a protectorate which two years later was consolidated into the British Central African Protectorate. The first Commissioner of the Protectorate, the fervid imperialist H.H. Johnstone, had no doubt about the cause of the Company's failure: . . . the riff-raff of Glasgow is not the best material with which to to develop the commerce of British Central Africa."[17]

But even in economic terms it was not all loss. The Moirs' pioneering laid the way for the commercial cultivation of tea, coffee and tobacco. And when the Company was taken over in 1893 by Cecil Rhodes' British South Africa Company, the latter acquired by the transaction two and three-quarter million African acres along with extensive mineral rights, many of which the Lakes' Company had acquired from local chiefs by methods which were a cause of scandal to the more tender among Victorian consciences.

The second major Scottish venture in eastern Africa—William Mackinnon's Imperial British East Africa Company—shared with the Lakes Company the feature of being short on economic success but long on political impact.

In 1871 Mackinnon's British India Company started a shipping service to the East Coast of Africa. The year before the formation of the Lakes Company—but from much the same mixture of commercial and missionary motives—Mackinnon extended his East Africa interest by giving the Indian Ocean merchanting firm of Smith, Mackenzie, in which he had been a partner since the 1850's, the East Africa agency for the British India Company. When ten years later Mackinnon formed the Imperial British East Africa Company, Smith, Mackenzie was one of the subscribers along with a selection of prominent businessmen which included A.A. Bruce, a son-in-law of Livingstone and a director of the Lakes Company, H.L. Younger, Bruce's partner in the Edinburgh brewing concern, and James Hutton of the Royal Niger Company. The Company won Chartered status in 1888 but like the Lakes Company failed to generate sufficient revenue to pay the heavy costs of combined economic pioneering and territorial administration in an area subject to growing international pressure. Mackinnon's appeal to the Government in 1893 for a £50,000 subsidy was rejected and the Government bought out the Company's rights for £200,000 and included the area in the East Africa Protectorate created in 1895.[17]

Scottish firms on the West Coast of Africa enjoyed greater economic success. The Glasgow firm of Miller and Brothers was a major force in the palm-oil trade in the 1860's and 1870's. Its River Niger interests were taken over by Sir George Goldie in 1879 and played a vital part in the development of the United Africa Company.

Along with a major holding by the Coats family, the Miller stake in the United Africa Company underpinned the 27% Scottish interest in the United Company's Chartered successor the Royal Niger Company. If its Royal Niger interests are included with its other interests, Miller's was the biggest single trading concern on the African West Coast in the 1880's and

1890's and was almost as big as all its Liverpool rivals taken together. But Miller's and the other Scottish firms on the West Coast like Taylor Laughland and Couper Johnstone in the palm-oil trade and W.B. McIver with its rubber and timber interests in Sierra Leone and the Gold Coast never organised themselves as a distinctive 'interest' in the way the Liverpool firms did through the Africa Association.[18]

It is impossible to compute the real volume of Scottish investment in the Third World in the nineteenth century. The wide variety and range of Scottish commercial enterprise, particularly in Asia, may give a misleading impression of the size of the capital commitment. Although some of the biggest firms like James Finlay acquired fixed assets in manufacturing, land or transport, the majority remained essentially traders and agents. While most Scottish enterprises in Asia, if not in Africa, appear to have yielded a good return for their stockholders, the Third World countries had formidable rivals as areas for Scottish investment. Probably the greater part of the estimated £500m of Scottish overseas investment by 1914 was located in the areas of white settlement, in North America, Australia and New Zealand, and South America.[19]

Scotland's commercial empire certainly stimulated the process of capital accumulation. But perhaps the chief benefit it brought to the Scottish enconomy was access to new markets. As merchants and agents Scottish firms were indispenable middlemen between producers and consumers in the different parts of the Empire. Of course few of the firms had homeward links exclusively with Scotland; as the century advanced London's financial dominance became more marked and Manchester led Glasgow as the main provider of the cotton piece goods which were such an important part of Imperial trade. Nevertheless the Scottish origins and connections of firms like James Finlay, Jardine Matheson, Mackenzie Mackinnon, Miller Brothers, the Bombay Burmah Trading Company, the Irrawaddy Flotilla Company and the several score of less illustrious Scottish trading houses, acted as a far-flung promotional and marketing service for Scottish industry. Scotland's producers of capital goods—her steelmakers, shipbuilders and marine engineers, her manufacturers of industrial machinery, her locomotive builders, her electrical and constructional engineers—were among the chief beneficiaries. But many other Scottish industries from textile to coal mining, from brewing and distilling to publishing, also benefitted from Scotland's informal commercial empire.

Little more than the skeleton survives today. A few familiar names are still there. James Finlay and Co. have added merchant banking, confectionery and North Sea services to their tea interest in India, Bangla Desh and Kenya. From their headquarters in Hong Kong Jardine Matheson boast that their 50,000 employees can provide almost every type of commercial service in Asia, the Pacific, the Middle East and Southern

Africa. Burmah Petroleum employs 28,000 people, although relatively few are now in the Third World. There have been some new arrivals in the ranks of Scottish international companies. Coats Paton which as J. and P. Coats began its overseas expansion in the United States in the 1860's, has established thread or textile manufacturing capacity in many Third World countries in the last four decades: today two-thirds of its 65,000 employees are outside the United Kingdom. Distillers Company with a turnover close to £900m. chiefly from whisky and other spirits, has markets in Asia, Africa and Latin America. United Biscuits, with its headquarters south of the Border but registered in Scotland, is an international food company with a turn-over in excess of £800m. Many smaller Scottish firms like the Weir Group, Low and Bonar and Anderson Strathclyde have important subsidiaries or associates in the Third World. And Scottish firms sell an estimated £1,000m. of goods there each year. But with the Scottish economy itself now dominated by foreign capital, the centre has collapsed and the lines of communication have been broken. Scotland, once the thrusting junior partner in the world's greatest Imperial venture, is herself now a colony of new economic empires.

References
1. Lythe S.G. and Butt J. *An Economic History of Scotland 1100-1939* Blackie 1975.
2. Orbell J. *From Cape to Cape. The History of Lyle Shipping* Paul Harris Edinburgh 1978.
3. Lenman B. *An Economic History of Modern Scotland* Batsford London.
4. Greenberg M. *British Trade and the Opening of China 1800-1842* Monthly Review Press New York and London 1951.
5. *James Finlay and Co. Ltd., Manufacturers & East India Merchants 1750-1950.* Published Jackson & Co. Glasgow 1951.
6. *Jardine Matheson and Co. A Historical Sketch* Jardine Matheson. Hong Kong (n.d.), Greenbery M. op. cit. and Allen G.C. and Donnethorne A.G. *Western Enterprise in Far Eastern Economic Development.* Allen and Unwin London 1962.
7. *Smith, Mackenzie and Company Ltd. A History* Smith, Mackenzie and Co. 1938 and W.H. Marwick *Economic Developments in Victorian Scotland,* Allen and Unwin 1938.
8. Laird D. *Paddy Henderson. The Story of P. Henderson and Co. 1834-1961* P. Henderson and Co. 1961.
9. Orbell J. op. cit.
10. Dictionary of National Biography 1931-1940 James Lyle Mackay (Lord Inchcape).
11. McCrae A. and Prentice A. *Irrawaddy Flotilla* James Paton Paisley 1978.
12. Stewart A.T.Q. *The Pagoda War: Lord Dufferin and the Fall of the*

Kingdom of Ava Faber and Faber London 1972.

13. Lenman B., Lythe C. and Gauldie E. *Dundee and its textile industry 1850-1914* Abertay Historical Society Publications No. 14, 1969. Walker E. *Juteopolis: Dundee and its textile workers 1885-1923* John Donald, Edinburgh 1981. Scott and Hughes *The Anatomy of Scottish Capital* Croom Helm, London 1980 pp 36-40.

14. Pontou A.C. *The Bombay Burmah Trading Coropration Ltd. 1863-1963* The Millbrook Press 1963.

15. Longhurst H.C. *The Borneo Story: The History of the First 100 Years of Trading in the Far East by the Borneo Company Ltd.* The Borneo Company 1956.

16. Macmillan H.W. *The Origin and Development of the African Lakes' Company* Ph.D. thesis University of Edinburgh 1970.

17. Smith, Mackenzie and Co. op. cit. and Galbraith J.S. *Mackinnon and East Africa: A Study of the New Imperialism* Cambridge 1972.

18. Thompson W. *Glasgow and Africa: Connexions and Attitudes 1870-1900* Ph.D. thesis University of Strathclyde 1970.

19. Lythe S.G. and Butt J. op. cit. p. 237.

MERCHANT CAPITAL
AND THE END OF EMPIRE:
JAMES FINLAY, MERCHANT ADVENTURERS

by Roger Jeffery

James Finlay and Company Ltd. is not the most obvious choice for close analysis in the context of capital in Scotland. While the company is of course a large Scottish company by turnover, it has a very small Scottish work-force, and in the field of merchant banking is by no means a dominant or typical firm.[1] The apparent perversity remains if the focus is placed on India, where Finlay firms were representatives of what Alavi calls 'old' rather than 'new' imperialism, with interests in the declining areas of jute and tea, rather than in mainstream Indian industries or the areas of new technology.[2]

Nevertheless, the firm remains of interest. It is one of the few remaining independent firms based in Scotland from among those which took advantage of the rise of a capitalist world market based in North-west Europe in the 18th century. It played a significant role in the development of some sectors of the Indian economy under British imperialism—a role in which Scottish capital was not always merely a junior partner to the English. James Finlay and Company remains one of the major multinational Scottish companies, in spite of its recent metamorphosis, with continuing substantial interests in Bangla Desh and in Kenya, and minor interests elsewhere. My own interest in the firm stems originally from looking at their remaining Indian and East African tea investments. What I want to do in this paper is to contribute to an understanding of the role of Scottish capital in the British Empire, to consider the impact of the company, especially in India, and to relate the self-description of the company as 'merchant adventurers' to discussions of the nature and impact of 'merchant capital'.

1. A BRIEF HISTORY OF THE FIRM

The company's official history traces the firm to its founder, the first James Finlay, who established a partnership trading in textiles in 1750.[3] When the Glasgow tobacco trade collapsed with the American War of Independence, textiles became the back-bone of the West of Scotland economy. James Finlay's son, Kirkman Finlay, was well placed to benefit from this shift, and took the firm from its minor position in 1790 to a leading one in the 1830's. In 1801, Finlay's was the largest cotton firm in Scotland. Kirkman Finlay expanded the export trade in cotton and piece goods, moved into manufacturing by opening three mills (at Catrine in Ayrshire and Deanston in Stirlingshire), and moved on to the British stage with his advocacy of the ending of the East India Company's monopoly on trade with the East. A series of partnerships with concerns in Manchester and Liverpool, as well as other Glasgow merchants, allowed the Finlay firm to expand its trade in cotton with Bombay, Calcutta, Canton and Nassau, as well as the U.S.A. and continental Europe. Kirkman Finlay himself was a prominent Glasgow citizen, being Lord Provost and M.P. in 1812 and holding a number of other offices before turning himself into a landed gentleman by investing in an estate in Argyllshire. When he withdrew to his castle, the firm nearly went bankrupt.

At this stage the firm was still basically a partnership. The expansion of the firm meant the introduction of new partners with new capital and vigour. John Muir and Hugh Brown fulfilled this function for the firm in the 1860's, and its modern incarnation can be said to date from this period. The Muir family, indeed, is still well represented in the upper echelons of the company. The new partners built up the business in cotton manufacturing and trading, and they were making over £150,000 a year in profit in the 1870's. The firm responded to the decline in the cotton trade in the 1880's by making new investments which set the face of the company for the following 80 years: investments in tea companies and in a steamer company plying between Britain and India.

It is not clear what prompted the move to invest in production outside Britain for the first time, nor why tea was chosen. Certainly, by this period, tea growing and manufacture were well established in Assam, and to a lesser extent in South India and Ceylon, though the days of the early pioneers, characterised by high profits followed by frequent bankruptcies, were over. The Finlay firm, with its established trading interests in Calcutta, was well placed to take advantage of the more settled conditions. Tea—and later, jute—were products where knowledge of the overseas markets probably gave considerable competitive advantage, and the Finlay partners saw this as their main speciality. In addition, other Scottish companies were following similar lines—for example, the Duncan partnerships—and many of the new planters and jute merchants were of Scottish origin, so there were perhaps ethnic forces pushing Finlay into similar fields.[4] John Muir seems to have been the driving force behind these moves.

By the end of the century, the locus of the firm was solidly in its India connections; as Scott and Hughes show, in 1904-5, the Finlay group was rather peripheral to the central business network in Scotland.[5] In spite of some kinship links with a branch of the Coats and Denny families, linking directorships outside the main Finlay companies were few. This pattern continued into the interwar and postwar periods: within the Finlay group, a small number of men held many directorships, but few of them held any position outside the group. The process of reorganisation of the whole

25

group around 1970 marks the first serious change.

Some idea of what the Finlay company was doing in India can be gleaned from the activities of its Calcutta branch, founded in 1870 and forming the backbone of the company's Indian operations.[6] To begin with, the branch traded in cotton textiles and as agents for insurance companies. Then it moved into other trading—rice, silk, and jute being exported and salt, beer and wine being imported. In 1872 a jute pressing mill was established, and the following year the Champdany Jute Co. was floated. The next steps were to expand the insurance and shipping agency work, and to take on the management of tea plantations. By the 1890's the Calcutta branch was also appointed agent to a railway company which served a major tea-growing area, as well as trading in indigo and holding agencies in coal mining (which did not last long) and in the management of a sugar company.

To some extent this was at the expense of local merchants: for example, the company took over a firm of jute traders in Narayanganj, who started as partners but who were increasingly bought up each time they had financial difficulties. The other expansions were part of the processes whereby the original owners of plantations were able to retire or expand into larger units by sub-contracting the management of their tea gardens to Calcutta-based firms of managing agents. The managing agency was an institution almost restricted to India, and there have been considerable disputes about the reasons for its use and impact.[7] Many companies did not have managing directors (sometimes no directors at all) but hired an agent (an individual, partnership or private company) to manage the affairs of the enterprise for them. Typically, the agent also promoted the company in the first place, and owned some of the shares: much criticism of the system focussed on the impossibility of real 'arms-length' negotiations between agents and companies in these situations, fostering a sense that the shareholders were being cheated. Since the managing agent received his fee whether or not the company made a profit, was free to buy from and sell to other companies he was managing, and held a contract which was almost impossible to abrogate, accusations of bad faith were common. However, managing agencies also had economies of scale; had access to sources of finance; and were a way of economising on scarce European managerial skills. (Indian managing agents, often much smaller, were probably generated in slightly different ways.) In consequence of this pattern, however, individual managing agents could come to control far more substantial capital resources than would be possible by other means.

Finlay's Indian branches used this pattern in the launching, and subsequent management, of four large tea planting companies in the 1890's— Consolidated Tea and Lands, Amalgamated, Anglo-American Direct and Kanan Devan—which bought up some of the companies already managed by Finlay branches in Calcutta and Colombo, as well as new land for planting. These companies were unusual: they were by far the largest tea companies operating in India and Ceylon (most other companies began with only one or two estates), and they were floated in the U.K. rather than on the Indian stock exchanges. These are the companies which elevate the Finlay group into the kind of prominence which they are accorded in 'The Anatomy of Scottish Capital', since it is control over these companies and ownership of their shares which gives it a substantial capital base. In India, the ranking of agencies by the rupee capital they controlled in the first half of the 20th century placed Finlay in a much lower position than it merited when these big Scottish companies were included.[8] For the moment I will focus on the effects of this kind of firm in India, before returning to consider the ways in which the firm has developed.

2. FINLAY IN INDIA

While the Finlay group looks peripheral to the Scottish context, this is far from the case when the focus is shifted to India. In spite of frequent comments in the firm's official history about the unprofitability of much that the firm attempted in India, in the 1930's the Finlay group (i.e. companies in which they had a dominant shareholding and those for which they were managing agents) was one of the four largest in India (see Table 1). It is notable that whereas two of the other very large European groups declined during the 1930's, the Finlay group maintained its existing size—which in this context means that they did not begin to de-invest from India in the face of the Depression and rising Indian nationalism.

TABLE 1

FIVE LARGEST BUSINESS GROUPS IN INDIA, 1931 AND 1939
Total paid-up capital in millions of rupees

GROUP	1931 INNER CIRCLE	OUTER CIRCLE	TOTAL	1939 INNER CIRCLE	OUTER CIRCLE	TOTAL
Tata	261	12	273	249	93	341
Andrew Yule	216	0.6	216	123	0.6	123
Inchcape	151	26	177	159	26	185
Finlay	103	3	106	107	3	110
Martin Burn	87	4	91	73	5	78

SOURCE: C. Markovits, 'Indian Business and nationalist politics from 1931 to 1939', Ph.D. Thesis, Cambridge University, 1978, Appendix 1.
'Inner circle' is those companies where the group either has a dominant shareholding or acts as managing agents; 'Outer circle' is those companies where control might be shared with other companies, or where a group has no obvious controlling shares but a substantial investment.

TABLE 2

TEN LARGEST TEA GROUPS, INDIA 1922 AND 1938

	1922			1938		
GROUP	ACREAGE CROPPED	CROP (M. LBS)	TRADING PROFIT £'000s	ACREAGE CROPPED	CROP (M.LBS)	TRADING PROFIT £'000s
James Finlay	83,706	38.2	1,087	95,065	50.7	867
P R Buchanan	7,103	3.2	79	11,057	6.4	60
Octavius Steel	31,055	12.9	307	29,241	13.8	168
Geo. Williamson	26,907	15.5	405	25,911	19.5	209
H L Turner	22,656	12.0	369	21,781	13.7	130
Walter Duncan	20,885	10.3	286	22,490	14.0	202
Alex Lawrie	19,518	12.8	373	19,889	14.5	167
McLeod Russel	17,897	7.8	171	17,524	11.4	128
R G Shaw	17,139	11.9	312	21,830	14.8	137
Begg Roberts	15,116	7.1	206			
Goodricke	13,533	6.2	189			
Harrisons				20,873	10.2	286
Planters				23,208	17.4	194
TOTAL ABOVE	275,515	137.9	3,784	308,869	186.4	2548
Finlay Group Share	33%	30%	31%	34%	31%	36%

SOURCE: *Tea Producing Companies,* Mincing Lane Tea Share Brokers Association, 1923 and 1939 (as reported in A. Lyon, *The political economy of tea*, M.A. thesis, Sociology Deartment, Edinburgh University, 1980.) Finlay Group share includes P.R. Buchanan, a closely related associate. Companies are grouped by London agents.

In this period they were by far and away the largest tea group, controlling nearly 13% of Indian acreage in the interwar period—almost three times as much as their nearest rivals (see Table 2). At around the same time they were also ranked 17th in terms of cotton textile manufacture, 13th in the production of sugar, and were 13th overall in terms of industrial assets controlled ('industrial' here defined to include jute interests).[9] By comparison with these other groups, Finlay controlled only eight, relatively large companies registered in India, whereas Andrew Yule's interests included 50 companies. Control of tea estates in India was fairly heavily dominated by a small number of sterling tea companies. All sterling companies together controlled about 55% of Indian production and area under tea in 1922, and about 60% in 1938.[10] Within this pattern of increasing concentration, the Finlay group increased its dominance, raising its share of acreage cropped, production of tea, and trading profit in this period.

Through its powerful position in the tea industry, Finlay played a considerable role in the way the plantation sector in India developed, in Assam and Cachar in the north-east and on the borders of Madras and Kerala in the south. (Finlay companies were relatively unimportant in North Bengal and around Darjeeling, the other major tea area). The plantation economy depended on the management of a poorly paid labour force, in North India predominantly imported from elsewhere on temporary, often penal, contracts.[11] In South India the Kanan Devan Hills Produce Co. owned an area equivalent to a small district, with nearly 30,000 acres under tea and additional surrounding property. As in other parts of Indian industry in which Finlay companies operated, an excess of labour was common, there was a low level of technology and little innovation, and few tasks involved a level of skill beyond what could be acquired rapidly on the job. This meant that employment could fluctuate rapidly to meet the changes in demand and problems caused by variations in the weather or in the supply of crucial raw materials. Wages were kept low by a number of mechanisms: in urban areas, and in the early period (up to the 1920's) on tea gardens, migrants left their wives and families behind, so that the cushion of rural incomes allowed employers to meet only the costs of reproduction of the workers themselves.[12] Family labour subsidised the employer, and this principle was maintained when families did join workers on tea estates: wage rates were settled on the understanding that a family was normally maintained by the earnings, on average, of about 1.75 workers: and 'spare' land on the estates was made available to workers for their own cultivation of staples like rice. In addition, labourers faced working hours much longer than those acceptable in the U.K. at this period, with workers in Bombay textile mills working an average 14.5 hour day in 1905.[13]

In the case of the tea plantations, the establishment of the industry in Assam from the 1840's onwards involved, as elsewhere, the clearing of tribal groups from their traditional areas of hunting and gathering—gathering which in the case of the Singhpo included the manufacture of tea from leaves gathered from wild bushes, and for a short period sold to the Assam Company.[14] Land for tea gardens was created by the exclusion of the Singhpo after their rebellion in 1845, and the grant of large tracts on preferential terms to speculative planters. Much of this land was surplus to tea requirements, often because it was poorly drained or otherwise unsuitable, and the tea companies controlled three times as much land in the 1920's as they had under tea, greatly limiting the land available to the Assamese for subsistence crop cultivation. Nevertheless the Assamese in the fertile Brahmaputra valley were relatively affluent compared with many other parts of India. As a result, they were unwilling to accept the appalling conditions for the labour force in the early period. Many recruits from the hilly tribal tracts of Bihar and Central India were induced with false promises to make the arduous journey to Assam, and a sizeable proportion died on the journey from inadequate provisions.[15] As the Finlay company history puts it, deadpan:[16]

"Roads were tracks at best, and transportation had to be done very largely by coolie porterage, which was both laborious and uncertain; sometimes food for the workers did not arrive."

Even in the relatively settled period when the Finlay companies were established (the 1890's) conditions remained almost unbelievably bad. The Governor of Assam eventually added his voice to those condemning the situation as one in which the workers' lives were of little concern to the managers, where the worker who attempted to escape from this form of exploitation was liable to be flogged and forced to return to his job, and where workers were recruited by a mixture of force and fraud.[17] A visiting team from the British T.U.C. described similar conditions in the late 1920's, pointing out that the geographical isolation of the estates weakened the position of the workers still further, and the social welfare of the workforce was ignored.[18] The situation for workers in Assam was probably worse than that in South India, in part because the ethnic distance between tea workers and the surrounding population was much smaller, and workers could more easily return to their villages.

Similar descriptions of the condition of tea estate labour in the 1940's suggest that improvements were slow. Deshpande demonstrated that the average worker's family depended on the earnings of children under 12 to keep incomes high enough to pay for the necessities of life.[19] Major E. Lloyd Jones, a doctor with the Indian Medical Service, noted the lassitude of the children on the estates, infant mortality rates of 3000 per 100,000 births and poor health standards resulting directly from malnutrition. Only malaria had been brought under control; the other water-borne and environmental diseases affecting the workforce went unchecked.[20]

After Independence in 1947, the major part of the industry remained in India, but the Sylhet estates (previously regarded as the poor relations of the Assam industry) were in East Pakistan (now Bangla Desh). In Pakistan, legislation which restricted the role of foreign capital was very slight, and few restraints were placed on the tea companies. In India, there was more political support for legislative action, and in 1951 a Plantations Labour Act was passed, regulating social provisions and opening the estates to union activities for the first time. Lloyd Jones expressed the rationale for the Act:[21]

"No-one would pretend that the labour was brought to the gardens for any reason than to increase the production of tea, and to bring profit to the tea owners. Since the labour is imported for this specific purpose, no reasonable person would deny that the owners who imported the labour have a moral responsibility to see that the labourers and their families are guaranteed a decent and human standard of living. Otherwise their condition would be reduced to one of mere slavery. It would be easy to make out a case for the contention that the condition of labour in years gone by has been very little if any better than slavery, but the moral obligation upon the owners still remains, even if many of them in the past have neglected to observe that obligation."

Since the passing of this Act, conditions in India have begun to improve, though real wage rates have been at best stable, showing a decline throughout the 1960's and early 1970's when profitability was low.[22] In Pakistan, where Finlay companies controlled some 30% of the industry, profits remained high in this period because the tea estates in East Pakistan (now Bangla Desh) had guaranteed markets in West Pakistan. But the condition of the workforce deteriorated. A study for the British Overseas Development Ministry in 1977 described a workforce whose low productivity was directly related to its poor nutritional standard, where the workers' housing was predominantly wattle-and-dub, where real incomes were declining, where little or no improvements had been carried out during the period of prosperity prior to 1971; and where the workforce was apathetic, malnourished and illiterate.[23]

Finlay were not merely represented in this industry, but played a very prominent role. The Finlay company comprised Scottish managers and investors, employing large numbers of Indians—the Calcutta office in 1939 controlled a workforce of nearly 140,000, of whom only 354 (0.25%) were European. The company history is in no doubt that this benefitted Indians:[24]

"The firm provided conditions, better than they had known, for a multitude of peasant workers, and created opportunities for the rapidly expanding Indian middle class . . . If more and better employment, more and better transport, more and better public health and education, more and better means of employment are good things, then James Finlay and Co. have served India well."

All of these claims can be challenged, not only with reference to the Bangladesh evidence summarised above, but also with respect to conditions on estates controlled by Finlay in India in the 1970's.[25] However, it is also clear that the Finlay group benefitted considerably from the contact with India, not just by 'doing as the Romans do' but also through its specific policies. Two areas are worthy of comment here: the company response to the problems of the Indian economy in the 1930's; and its involvement in the International Tea Agreement of the 1930's and 1940's.

31

The Indian economy in the inter-war period faced considerable difficulties, in part the result of the world depression but also because of features peculiar to India—policies decided in London by the colonial government were slow to provide protection and patronage to Indian industries, for example.[26] In some areas both Indian and British industries suffered, with Japanese exports of cotton goods destroying the Indian export markets in China, and increasingly replacing Lancashire as the major source of imports into India. Jute, after the war-time boom, faced dire problems of over-capacity, and attempted to cope by restricting output, though there was never a workable agreement. In tea, a voluntary agreement in 1930 was replaced by the first International Tea Regulation Scheme in 1933. Thus in all of the major sectors in which the Finlay group was involved, there were considerable problems.

This period, of course, also saw the rise of Indian nationalism, with an increasingly activist and mass line under Gandhi's leadership, and the growth of an Indian bourgeoisie based on profits earned during the First World War. There was considerable hostility in the business community to the Government moves which transferred increasing amounts of political control to Indians in 1919 and 1935.[27] Several of the largest European managing agencies began to disinvest in this period, bringing in Indian partners or selling their holdings in some subsidiary companies, and there was a general unwillingness to make new investments.[28] While the Finlay group responded in part by looking elsewhere for investment opportunities, it was unusually willing to consider new capital expenditure on its textile interests, changing over to finer cotton production and electrifying its jute mills.[29] In tea, a different policy was followed. With other companies (notably Brooke Bond) it searched out land in East Africa, buying 20,000 acres in 1925 for $60 (!) and a yearly rental on a 999 year lease of £200.[30] By 1934 the Finlay company (African Highlands Produce) had over 5000 acres of mature tea, about 40% of Kenya's total, with Brooke Bond controlling another 40%. There followed a battle for the East African market, which Brooke Bond won easily, using its extensive U.K. marketing experience. As before (with Anglo-American Direct, which, in spite of its name, never really established a position in the U.S.A.), the Finlay group remained in production and not marketing, a position it keeps today.

As a result of these developments, Finlay companies were heavily involved in the negotiations for an International Tea Agreement both in 1933 and on its renewal in 1938.[31] The Finlay group was prominent in representing planters in India and Ceylon, and the London agents, because its managers were chairmen of the Indian Tea Associations in London and Calcutta, and convened the Colombo committee established to deal with the question.[32] The scheme adopted in 1933 restricted output on the basis of the historic shares of world trade of the countries concerned; which meant that the newer areas like Kenya found their expansion plans severely constrained. Nevertheless, the Kenyan Government joined the scheme, on the advice of the Kenya Tea Growers Association—not very surprising, given that the KTGA was dominated by Brooke Bond and Finlay, more concerned for their Indian investments at this time. By 1938, the smaller Kenyan growers had sufficient influence to force the Kenyan Government to withdraw from the scheme until the restrictions on the output of their growers were removed; and after the Second World War Kenya withdrew completely. By this time, the significance of the Kenyan estates to companies like Brooke Bond and Finlay was growing, and in a context where planters from India were looking for an escape hole to avoid having to work under an independent Indian Government there was little danger that the Kenyan industry would suffer unduly.[33]

It is not immediately obvious why the Finlay group maintained and even extended its position in India during the inter-war years. If profitability is any guide to policy, it is clear that Finlay group companies, in tea at least, came through the Depression fairly well. Once the uncertainty caused by the First World War was over, dividends paid by most companies in the period 1922-27 were excellent, with the average for all tea companies ranging between 20% and 37% in these years. Even in the 1930's returns were not as bad as might have been expected (see Table 3). By maintaining its position in this way, the Finlay group was able to benefit considerably during the boom conditions of the Second World War: in the 10 years 1938-1947, the average rates of return to shareholders in the Finlay group Indian cotton mills was over 13%, and around 9% in jute investments, while the tea interests continued to do well.[34]

TABLE 3

DIVIDEND PAYMENTS BY TEA COMPANIES, 1914-1939

Company	1914-18	1919-23	1924-33	1937	1939
Amalgamated	9.4	12	10.9	7.0	7.0
Anglo-American	n.a.	n.a.	n.a.	n.a.	n.a.
Consolidated	n.a.	n.a.	16.75	13.0	10.0
Kanan Devan	n.a.	n.a.	24.5	16.0	14.5
All Indian tea companies	n.a.	16.3	15.9	12.6	n.a.

Source: V.D. Wickizer, *Tea under International Regulation*, Stanford, 1944, pp. 63 & 124-5

For whatever reasons, it is clear that the company avoided any contamination by Indian capitalist interests. Most of the Finlay interests by now were in Calcutta, where the capitalist class was much more heavily

European-dominated than in Bombay; and the company controlled units in the tea industry too large for easy disposal to Indian interests, though this is not true for the cotton and jute undertakings. The fact remains that the Finlay group did not bring Indians onto the boards of companies it managed until well after Independence, whereas in India as a whole the Indian involvement in the larger Indian companies rose from about 30% in 1918 to about 60% by 1939[35].

3. THE RESPONSE TO POLITICAL INDEPENDENCE

The Finlay group thus entered the post-war period very much as it had entered the period following the First World War, with only the Kenyan tea interests marking a substantial change from 1918. Again unusually, the changes in response to Indian Independence were restrained. Several of the big managing agencies were taken over by Indian interests, Andrew Yule being a prime example. Others shed their undertakings slowly, repatriating themselves to the U.K. or transferring their businesses to other parts of the Empire, with several other tea plantation companies following Finlay and Brooke Bond to East Africa. The Finlay group seems to have been much slower in reducing the scale of its investments. While the jute and cotton mills were sold fairly early, the tea interests (all registered in the U.K. and therefore less vulnerable to takeover pressures) remained in Finlay hands and in some cases expanded their acreages (see Table 4). The major exception was in the case of Amalgamated, which sold its Bangladesh and Sri Lankan interests in the mid-1950's.

TABLE 4

CULTIVATED ACREAGES OF FINLAY TEA COMPANIES IN SOUTH ASIA, 1948 to 1968

Company	1948	1958	1968
1. Amalgamated	16,080	7,568	6,846
2. Anglo-American	19,150	18,271	15,172
3. Consolidated	35,141	31,104	33,174
4. Kanan Devan	29,295	28,363	24,419
5. Chubwa	3,916	4,219	4,207
6. Achabam	600	680	786
7. Baraoora	4,357	4,470	5,289
8. Borhat	1,650	1,798	1,045
9. Chargola	2,951	0	0
10 Noyapara	835	941	993
TOTAL	113,975	97,432	91,913

Source: *Stock Exchange Yearbook*, relevant years. Nos. 6-10 were managed by P.R. Buchanan. Figures include acreages under coffee and spices. The various companies had different (and probably varying) holdings by the Finlay Group.

The company began its transformation to its current structure in the mid-1960's.[36] To begin with, the Deanston cotton mill was closed, followed soon after by the closing of the mill in Catrine. By 1971 the company had severed its links with the villages which formed the basis of its Scottish activities for 150 years, leaving only the merchant banking and agency work apart from the tea interests. At this point the tea companies were reorganised, with the formation of new holdings companies which provided greater protection from takeover interest (manifested around 1970 by the shareholding of the Slater group which rose to over 20% of James Finlay at one period). The relationship with McLeod Russel, also substantial shareholders in the tea companies, was tense for a while, but by 1973 the new structure was established, with Finlay's Indian holdings in tea being mediated by the Cessnock, Teith and West Nile Holdings Companies.

In retrospect, these arrangements were but a prelude to a rapid divestment of interest in tea companies in India. In 1973 the Indian Government passed a Foreign Exchange Regulation Act, which provided (amongst other things) for the progressive dilution of expatriate holdings in Indian companies. The implementation of this Act took some time; it did not apply equally to all sectors of the Indian economy, and the tea companies were able to raise the limit of foreign holding for them from the general ceiling of 40% to a 76% limit. But most foreign companies took this Act as an indicator of the future pattern in which their holdings would be steadily whittled away, and the companies whose world-wide policy forbad this (e.g. Coca-Cola and I.B.M.) were forced to abandon their fight and withdraw from India altogether. Most tea companies have responded by setting up Indian associates in which they hold a majority of the shares, but the Finlay companies were transferred in a different way. In the early 1970's the Finlay group had established a small instant tea production company in collaboration with Tata, one of the two largest Indian multinational conglomerates. In 1976, through a complex financial procedure, all Finlay's Indian tea interests were sold to this company (Tata-Finlay), in exchange for a 20% share in the new company and £3.6 million, paid over the following 5 years. McLeod Russel also have a 20% stake in the new company, which controls about 8% of Indian production and is by far the largest tea production company in India. Since 1980 the next largest group of Indian companies, controlled through Camellia Holdings by a Canadian, Gordon Fox, living in Cannes, has followed a similar path in transferring its resources out of India.[37]

The distribution of Finlay's turnover has thus changed dramatically (see Table 5). The company has drastically reduced its plantation interests in Asia, and replaced them (after an unsuccessful foray into the North American market) with new investments in the U.K., especially related to North Sea oil interests. The timing of this shift was, in retrospect, exceptionally poorly judged: 1977 and 1978 were bumper years for the tea companies

TABLE 5

DISTRIBUTION OF FINLAY TURNOVER 1968, 1973 and 1978

By type of activity	1968	1973	1978
1. Plantations	91%	50%	20%
2. Merchant Banking	0.3%	4%	—
3. Manufacturing: foodstuffs			33%
	8%	32%	
4. Other manufacturing, servicing and merchanting			40%
5. International confirming and finance	2%	8%	7%

By geographical area			
Asia	45%	24%	23%
Africa	30%	25%	23%
North America	0.1%	17%	6%
Australasia	1%	4%	4%
United Kingdom	23%	30%	47%

Source: James Finlay and Co. Ltd, *Annual Reports,* relevant years. The system of classification changed in 1976, so the 1978 figures are not strictly comparable with the earlier years.

and the company lost a good share of the profits which were earned in India on estates which they had previously owned. In addition, the weaknesses of the new investments were made abundantly clear by the sources of profits in these years. In spite of its small share in turnover, the plantation sector provided the bulk of the profits, over 60% in 1977 and 1978. Company statements suggest that it would like to withdraw from Bangladesh, if there were any potential buyers and if the company could be assured of repatriating the results of the sale; but the Kenyan interests are more protectively viewed, and contribute far more to the overall profit.

4. CONCLUSION

The Finlay group has, in many respects, followed an unusual trajectory for Scottish companies which were established and developed on the back of English Imperialism. Unlike Jardine Matheson, for example, control over the company remained firmly in Scotland; unlike the Irrawaddy Flotilla Company, it survived world-wide depression and the collapse of the political empire. Its nearest equivalent is probably Burmah Oil, but the Finlay Group managed the transfer of its main investments back to the U.K. rather more successfully than Burmah did. Even now, when the focus of its activities are within the U.K. (and especially within Scotland) it is still taking on new investments in its traditional stamping grounds—tourism in Sri Lanka being a recent example.

Superficially, the company can be regarded as a classic case of merchant capital: indeed, the company chairman, Sir Colin Campbell is proud of the title, as he made clear in 1979:[38]

> "We are merchant adventurers and go to seek a fortune for our stockholders in many parts of the world, and when in Rome we do as the Romans do."

Geoff Kay has attempted to analyse the nature of underdevelopment in terms of the impact of merchant capital on peripheral economies, and at first glance the Finlay group falls neatly into the category.[39] The 'managing agency' system is obviously one in which merchant rather than industrial principles could be expected to hold, and the early history in trade might reinforce this view. However, closer analysis demonstrates some problems. To begin with, as Kay himself notes, for Marxists merchant capital can add nothing to the value of the commodities it handles, and is supposed thereby to be incapable of effecting a transition to capitalism—yet he goes on to argue that merchant capital was forced out of the sphere of circulation into production around the end of the 19th century in the colonies. Part of his argument rests on claiming that plantation agriculture was not 'really' capitalist, because of its reliance on migrant labour (coerced by non-economic mechanisms) and because it had a low degree of capitalisation.[40] It is obviously difficult to make any statements about a category such as 'merchant capital' on the basis of an individual example, but it seems hard to account for the varying patterns of Finlay's activities as simply as that. The company always had a manufacturing base in textiles, both in Scotland and India, and undertook a variety of other industrial activities in India before 1947. The particular form of that investment—the managing agency —has been a very contentious issue among historians, but currently there seems some consensus that it was not an inhibitory but a helpful force in the growth of Indian industry.[41]

But the impact on India of its tea industry is also contentious. Certainly the tea areas are now heavily dependent on a dying world market in which international competition has a distinct advantage. The Indian work-force remains poorly paid, undernourished, largely illiterate and often diseased—and this condition is unlikely to improve with Indian capitalist control or through State intervention. The legacy of the tea industry is increasingly a burden which needs to be lightened—even if the effects in India are less dramatic than in Sri Lanka. However, little seems to be gained by calling either the originators or the inheritors of the estates 'merchant capitalists'.[42]

As for its impact on Scotland, again a qualified judgement seems in order. The firm was part of the process whereby capital moved out of Scotland in the latter part of the 19th century, and in the early 20th century the company played its part in the downfall of the Dundee jute industry through its sponsorship of a Calcutta-based competition. On the other hand, the profits remitted to Scotland have helped the maintenance of a Scottish rentier class, and returned tea planters have been a sizeable element in that class—though I know of no estimates of their significance. Even in the manner of their return to Scotland, as Scott and Hughes note, they are merely playing a financial role not unlike the role they have played in many other parts of the world. In this sense, then, they can be regarded as 'merchants' in that they are concerned with a shorter term than many of their industrial competitors, and that they carry a much smaller managerial structure than, for example, Brooke Bond.[43] This may mean that they are better suited to the nature of modern Britain, having shed their increasingly anachronistic character ten years ago; but it will not make Scots any more proud of Finlay's contribution to their society.

References

1. In 1978, Finlay was the 6th largest Scottish-registered company by pre-tax profits and was 17th in terms of sales, but this was an exceptional year because of high tea prices: *Scotland's Top 500 Companies 1978*, London 1978. The company rose from a position around 700 in *The Times 1000* in 1972-3 to around 450 in 1980-81.

2. H. Alavi, 'Imperialism Old and New', *Socialist Register*, 1964.

3. *James Finlay & Company Limited*, Glasgow, 1951. The following paragraph draws heavily on this source.

4. *The Duncan Group*, London, 1959; see also H. Bolitho, *James Mackay, First Lord Inchcape*, London, 1934.

5. J. Scott & M. Hughes, *The Anatomy Of Scottish Capital*, London 1980.

6. *James Finlay*, op. cit.

7. See P.S. Lokanathan, *Industrial Organisation in India*, London, 1935; M.M. Mehta, *The Structure of Indian Industries*, Bombay, 1955; R.S. Rungta, *The Rise of Business Corporations in India, 1850-*

1900, Cambridge, 1970; R.K. Ray, *Industrialisation in India*, Delhi, 1979; M.D. Morris, *'Modern Business. Organisation and Labour Administration'*, E.P.W. (Bombay), 1979, 1680-7.

8. Compare Ray, op. cit. pp 260-1 with Table 1 below.

9. Markovits, op. cit.

10. Lyon, op. cit.

11. General information is available in P.J. Griffiths, *The History of the Indian Tea Industry*, London, 1967, but this almost completely ignores the managing agencies in an account very close to company propaganda.

12. G. Myrdal, *Asian Drama*, London, 1968, p.1106.

13. ibid., p.1107.

14. K. Deb, 'Impact of plantations on the agrarian structure of the Brahmaputra valley', Centre for Studies in Social Science Occasional paper no. 24, Calcutta, 1979.

15. Rungta, op. cit., p.100; *Papers regarding the tea trade*, Calcutta, 1870.

16. *James Finlay*, op. cit., p.107.

17. A. Guha, *Planter Raj to Swaraj*, Calcutta, 1976.

18. A.A. Purcell & J. Hallsworth, *Report on labour conditions in India*, London, 1928, pp.34-5.

19. S.R. Deshpande, *Report on an inquiry into the cost and standard of living of plantation workers in Assam and Bengal*, Delhi, 1948.

20. E. Lloyd-Jones, *Standards of Medical care for tea plantations in India*, Delhi, 1947, p.5.

21. ibid., p.41.

22. see J. Tanner (ed.), *The Tea Trade*, London, 1979, p.8.

23. J.D. Pell et al., *Rehabilitation project for the Bangladesh Tea Industry* Report of a mission financed by the Overseas Development Ministry, London, 1977.

24. *James Finlay*, op. cit., pp.115 & 125.

25. Tanner (ed.), op. cit., p.9.

26. A.K. Bagchi, *Private Investment in India 1900-39*, Cambridge, 1972; Ray, op. cit.

27. B.R. Tomlinson, *The Political Economy of the Raj 1914-1947*, London, 1979.

28. Ray, op. cit.

29. *James Finlay*, op. cit. pp.112 & 117.

30. N. Swainson, in R. Kaplinsky (ed.), *The Multinational Corporation in Kenya*, Nairobi, 1978.

31. V.D. Wickizer, *Tea under International Regulation*, Stanford, 1944.

32. *James Finlay*, op. cit., p.109.

33. Swainson, op. cit.

34. Mehta, op. cit., pp.84-6; see also Table 6 below.

35. Ray, op. cit.

36. See the Annual Reports, 1968 onwards, for data reported in this paragraph.

37. *'Tea: Not-so-strange case for Jokai India'*, E.P.W., 1979, 1788-9.

38. *Glasgow Herald*, 30 July 1979.

39. G. Kay, *Development and Underdevelopment*, London, 1975.

40. ibid.

41. Morris, op. cit.

42. For further discussion of this, see the review of Kay by Henry Bernstein, *Review of African Political Economy*, 1976.

43. To some extent this is hearsay evidence, but also from research in Kenya by L. Lee and J. Henley.

James Finlay Merchant Adventurers

APPENDIX

TABLE 6

DIVIDENDS PAID BY MAJOR FINLAY COMPANIES 1941-70

Company	1941-45	1946-50	1951-55	1956-60	1961-65	1966-70
Amalgamated	7.8*	15.2	5.5	7.5	9.0	9.5
Anglo-American	9.4*	21.1	18.1	14.0	13.5	5.0*
Consolidated	11.25*	21.5	11.2	18.0	25.0	38.5*
Kanan Devan	13.9*	21.2	14.5	12.5	10.0	2.5*
					12.8	
James Finlay	13.6	25.0	8.2	9.6		14.0

Source: *Stock Exchange Yearbook,* relevant years. Figures are annual averages of 5 years, except for those starred, which are of 4 years only. Because of changes in tax regulations, these figures are not strictly comparable.

41

COATS PATONS:
A SCOTTISH COMPANY IN INDIA

by Alan Sinclair

INTRODUCTION

Coats Patons is the most multinational of all Scotland's multinational companies. It operates in over 30 countries, spread over six continents, and manufactures 20% of all the thread sold in the world.

The company started more than 100 years ago in a room and kitchen in Paisley. In the decades which followed the town and the company grew together. But today, at the Company's Glasgow headquarters, Coats Patons management are spinning plans which provoke the wry comment in Paisley that the company's local operations will soon be back once more in a room and kitchen.

In 1960, J. & P. Coats employed 14,000 people in Paisley: today, that number has fallen to 1,400, with a further reduction of at least 700 jobs planned in the next two years. A similar contraction of Coats Patons' work-force and production levels is taking place not only in Scotland but all over Europe, while at the same time the company has been expanding its operations in Asia and South America.

At a time when the air is full of talk and speculation about employment and economic recovery, it is useful to cut through the pious expressions of hope for the future, and take a look at what one of the prime movers on the Scottish industrial scene is actually doing. Coats Patons may be one of Scotland's largest companies, and one of the most successful in international terms, but if hopes for economic recovery are based on the operations of companies like Coats Patons, they are likely to be severely frustrated.

In 1980, Coats Patons had total world sales of £689 million and profits of £66.4 million. The simultaneous rise of Coats Patons in the international sphere, and its decline in its own backyard, is due in large measure to its development as a multinational company. Of its £66.4 million profit in 1980, £56.3 million (79%) was contributed by its overseas operations. Its failure to secure adequate profit from its investments in the U.K. is striking.

The key figure to understand in the table following refers to the U.K. assets, which amount to 35.2% of the company's total assets, and yet yielded only 20.8% of profits in 1980. By contrast, the collective assets of Third World producers (South America, Africa and Asia) plus Australia, accounts for only 26.5% of total company assets and yielded 45.7% of profits.

Distribution of Turnover, Assets and Profit 1980

	Turnover £ millions	% of total	Assets Employed £ millions	% of total	Profit before Tax and Loan Interest £ millions	% of total
U.K.	251	36.4%	145	35.2%	15	20.8%
Europe	146	21.2%	84	20.4%	12	16.6%
N. America	117	16.9%	75	18.2%	12	16.6%
S. America	81	11.7%	54	13.6%	21	29.1%
Africa, Asia & Australia	94	13.6%	53	12.9%	12	16.6%
TOTAL (£)	689		411		72	

(The table is adapted from Coats Patons Annual Report 1980)

To put it more simply, one quarter of Coats Patons investments are in the southern hemisphere (mainly in the Third World). This quarter of their assets yields almost half (47.5%) of profits. Total U.K. assets amounted to £145.3 million in 1980, and produced a total profit of £15.2 million—which expressed as a percentage of profits over assets means a rate of return of 10.5%. Total assets employed in the Third World plus Australia for the same period amounted to £106.2 million and profits of £32.7 million, a return of 30.8%. Therefore the Third World investment yields almost three times as much profit per pound invested as the U.K. investment. That being the case, it is easy enough to understand the present trend of Coats Paton investment, which is to contract in the U.K. and Europe and expand in Asia and Latin America.

The pattern of opportunism established by Coats Patons in pulling out of the U.K. is matched by the story of its operations in its new production bases overseas. In this essay we take a close look at one part of Coats Patons' world-wide network, the Indian associate Madura Coats, which employs 22,000 people in the South of India. The investigation of Madura Coats' operation raises questions which Coats Patons should be required to answer; and it also presents a challenge to trade unions, international development aid organisations, and the public.

While Coats Patons' international network is currently giving employment to some 22,000 people in India, it is probable that the introduction of highly sophisticated textile production processes into what was, until relatively recently, a subsistence economy has destroyed the livelihoods of hundreds of thousands of primitive thread-makers and handloom weavers. Even for

43

those fortunate enough to obtain employment in a Madura Coats plant, there are considerable hardships and problems.

The three major trade unions in India, which might be expected to protect the workers' interests, have become corrupt and ineffective, largely as a result of the management's policy of ensuring the co-operation of union officials by giving them a certain number of jobs to dispose of at their own discretion. These are usually sold for handsome sums; workers have been known to hand over the equivalent of three years' wages in return for a desperately-needed job.

Health and safety records are not kept, and even the company's Personnel Manager agreed that conditions were "very poor" in comparison with similar plants in Europe. And although Madura Coats workers are reasonably well paid in Indian terms, the value of their labour to the company is such that in 1980, Madura Coats was able to repatriate £500,000 to the U.K. headquarters of Coats Patons in the form of a 20% dividend to shareholders, and contract fees. In the same year, Oxfam spent £1 million in India, a priority area for its work. In other words, Madura Coats **alone** sent back to the U.K. one-half of what Oxfam was able to put in. When it comes to providing generously for people on the other side of the world, the Madura Coats employee—working a 48-hour week for £12 so that Madura Coats can send massive profits back to the U.K.—has little to gain from the well-off Westerner who gives a few pounds to a Third World charity.

HISTORY
1900-1949

At the turn of the century, British textile manufacturers were in their heyday. Out of this group, two sewing-thread companies began to set up overseas—the Lancashire group, English Sewing Cotton (later to become Tootal) and J. & P. Coats of Paisley. For 50 years, J. & P. Coats concentrated on expanding in the U.S.A., Europe, the Commonwealth and Central and Southern America.

J. & P. Coats and Tootal were both masters of thread-making, which is regarded as a specialised branch of textile technology. The quality of the finished thread was of increasing importance with the growing use of automatic sewing machines pioneered by Singer.

A series of mergers before the turn of the century left the British market divided between the two domestic giants—both of which figured among the world's top 100 companies in the era before the First World War. As the British market was limited, and growth would only come with increases in consumer expenditure, both companies looked to overseas markets. At that time, the main markets were the developed industrialised countries, with large clothing and soft furnishing industries. Import tariff barriers existed to protect domestic industries, but these were overcome by setting up production facilities inside the countries concerned.

Whatever market Coats or English Sewing Thread chose to operate in, they offered formidable competition to local manufacturers, operating on a scale that dwarfed their competitors.

1950-1969

The decade after World War II found Coats consolidating its position as the world's leading specialist in sewing-thread manufacture, and adapting its production to the introduction of synthetic threads. The economic growth of that decade, with rising consumption, caused an increase in demand for thread products. J. & P. Coats was sufficiently well-diversified internationally to pick up the benefits of the new "miracle" economies like Japan and Hong Kong, and to avoid dependence on U.K. and U.S.A. markets.

In business, the guiding principle is always to make money—money not just for today but for tomorrow. In general, the 1960's were a time for heeding the old wife's advice—"Don't put all your eggs in one basket". For J. & P. Coats that meant, on top of its diverse international product range, diversifying out of thread and into other products.

By the end of the 1960's its textile interests embraced thread, woollen and synthetic yarns and fabrics, garment manufacturing and retailing, and it had diversified into engineering—particularly diecasting, plastic mouldings and zip-fastener manufacture. The route of acquisitions was as follows.

In 1960 J. & P. Coats acquired Paton and Baldwin, and formed the overall holding company of Coats Paton. Paton and Baldwin was considered a good fit—it supplied wool to industry and the home-knitting market, it had a big domestic marketing network and a small international sales network. J. & P. Coats had a small domestic network and a large international system— a good business marriage.

Next Passold's, the "Ladybird" children's wear firm, was bought. It was seen as a market innovator in producing and selling modern children's clothes in Britain. It also strengthened the British marketing operation.

A series of acquisitions occurred around 1967: Donaldson's Dalkeith, Jaeger, Herbert and Driver, Byford, Camelbank Hosiery, Laird Portch Fashions, John Heathcoat, and West Riding Worsted and Woollen. This round of company-buying made sense on two fronts: it integrated into the

Coats Patons: A Scottish Company in India

Coats Paton "family" various wool producers, which meant that one Coats Paton company could now sell wool to another which would turn it into garments, rather than selling it to independent third parties; and secondly, through Jaeger, Scotch Wool Shops and a new line, Country Casuals, Coats Paton could go into the High Street and do its retailing direct.

But the company was intent on spreading risks even wider through diversification outwith textiles.

It chose to concentrate on investing in integrated and automated processes for diecasting small metal parts, ranging from watch parts to moulds for plastic. Coats opened Dynacast in N. America, and later brought it to the U.K. Zip Fasteners were the other engineering product into which Coats Patons moved. By 1972, £35 million of turnover was coming from engineering—a larger turnover than well known engineering concerns like Harland and Wolff or Alfred Herbert.

1970-80

In its diversification phase in the 1960's, and again in the 70's and 80's Coats Patons, like Topsy, just growed and growed. From 1967 to 1972, thread sales increased by two-thirds. Changes continue to take place—closures and selling of shares were carried out in the Netherlands, where wage costs were considered too high; in Japan, where there was too much low cost competition; and in Chile, where Coats and the Allende government did not mix—although today, Coats Patons are back in the Chile of General Pinochet with a 64% holding in Cia. Ind. Hilos Cadena S.A. Factories were opened in Spain, Portugal, Malaysia, Hong Kong, Brazil, Thailand, Indonesia and the Philippines. In the first instance, the opening up of production in Third World countries seems to have been motivated by the need to duck protectionist trade barriers by supplying the market from within. However, at a second stage, such plants have been used to export to other markets.

Today Coats Patons has a work force of 60,000 with 20,000 employed in the U.K. and 40,000 scattered over the world. The table below illustrates the institutional and private mix typical of modern industrial ownership. Although Mr. W.D. Coats is the company chairman, individual shareholdings only account for 26% of the company's ownership. Banks, Insurance Companies, Investment Trusts and Pension funds make up the bulk of the owners: the single biggest holding, a 6% stake, is held by the Prudential Insurance Company. In what has been a difficult time for U.K. textile companies Coats Patons' share prices have suffered but largely thanks to its international spread it has weathered the storm.

46

Coats Patons: A Scottish Company in India

HOW THE GIANT OPERATES

Despite diversification, Coats Patons' biggest earner remains industrial and home sewing thread. With thread production plants in 30 countries, Coats Patons operates a "Group Best Practice" in monitoring on a monthly basis the performance of each plant.

Imagine a national electricity grid converted to thread and organised on a world scale. Effectively that is what Coats Patons operates from its Glasgow headquarters. The thread produced by Madura Coats in India in 1980 measured 91,982 million metres, enough thread to wrap round the earth 2,000 odd times, pole to pole. And then there are all the other Coats Patons thread producing plants in 30 other countries, each plant pumping out a certain measure of thread, with a certain capacity kept back in store. A few words across the telex or telephone and a part of the grid flies into action, the same international "scissors" cutting off the supply when enough thread has been produced.

In deciding where to allocate production on a short term basis, and where in the longer term to site new investment, and thus maximise the opportunities afforded by the "thread grid", Coats Patons uses a formula to calculate relative costs of production. The formula includes exchange rates, national insurance costs, rates of pay and productivity. With this information to hand the company has the knowledge to match its capability of shifting production to the lowest cost centres. Set out below is a table illustrating rates of pay for twelve countries.

Shareholders and Shareholding

	Number	% of ordinary shareholders
Insurance companies	185	18.6%
Investment trusts and institutions	881	11.8%
Pension funds	126	10.9%
Nominee companies	172	6.8%
Limited companies	176	0.3%
Banks and bank nominee companies	1,991	25.4%
Individual accounts	46,756	26.2%

Coats Patons Annual Report 1980

Coats Patons: A Scottish Company in India

Comparative Labour Costs

	SINGLE SHIFT Total Cost £1/Hr.	Index
U.K.	2.678	100
ITALY	3.259	122
W. GERMANY	3.561	133
CANADA	3.596	134
U.S.	3.134	117
PORTUGAL	1.076	40
COLUMBIA	0.985	36
BRAZIL	0.840	31
PERU	0.611	23
INDIA	0.342	13
PHILIPPINES	0.276	10
INDONESIA	0.166	6

Financial Times, June 29th 1981

Investment decisions are not, however, simple. For example in April 1981, labour costs in India were 13% of U.K. labour costs. But the Glasgow H.Q. in deciding where to invest may decide to put money into the U.S. rather than India, as capital intensive investment in the USA will cut the U.S. labour force and thus reduce a costly item in the company's bill.

Although as the above example illustrates, high labour costs do not necessarily mean less investment, the pattern of investment demonstrated by Coats Patons' actions and articulated by their management indicates an increasing trend towards overseas investment:

"We follow growth. Our investment will inevitably be foreign, and our rationalisation will inevitably be in the EEC."

(Mr. W.R. Henry, former Chairman of Coats Patons, quoted in the Financial Times, 29.6.81.)

It is not simply that investment is not going into British textile mills, and that Coats Patons is no longer exporting from the U.K. to the countries to which it previously exported. Coats Patons is engaging in production from "platforms" in other countries and exporting from there into the EEC and the U.K.

The company has now joined the bandwagon it once criticised:

"No-one should defend inefficiency, but it must be pointed out that a considerable part of our old industries is not efficient. The

48

textile industry, which is labour intensive, is a good example. The Multi-Fibre Arrangement, which establishes quotas for imports from the Far East—where wages are between 6% and 25% of U.K. wages—creates an impossible level of competition to a U.K. manufacturer, as the wage gap is too great to be bridged by the very highest level of efficiency."

(Mr. W.R. Henry, in his Chairman's Report, the Coats Patons Annual Report, 1979.)

What happens to Paisley?

The consequences of the drift to produce internationally have bitten deep in Scotland. In 1960, J. & P. Coats employed 14,000 people in Paisley: by November 1981 the total was down to 1,000 and falling further. In November of 1981 J. & P. Coats announced the cutting back nationwide of another 1,000 jobs in the next two to three years. The Ferguslie Mill at Paisley is to close and the future of the Anchor Mill hangs in the balance. The probable course of action for the Anchor Mill as outlined by the management, is for the Mill to concentrate exclusively on supplying core-spun industrial thread to the garment making industry and the consequent ending of hank processing and domestic household thread production.

The number of jobs in Paisley is expected to decline to 750 with the ending of production of two of its present products. Although Coats is giving up production of domestic household thread that does not mean that it is giving up its share of the market. In future that share of the market will be supplied by thread carrying the Coats name and symbols but "sourced" from outside the U.K. The thread may be purchased from other producers in the U.K. and then resold, but it is much more likely, considering Coats international "thread-grid" and the evidence from the case study of Coats in India, that the thread will be produced in an overseas part of the Coats Patons grid, and sold in the U.K.. Company strategy has turned a full circle. Moving out from the U.K. to avoid tariff walls and in some occasions to take advantage of cheap labour, Coats now supplies the British market while British manufacturing contracts.

Many of the job losses have occurred as a result of new technology. A study by the Overseas Development Institute on U.K. job losses in textiles between 1970 and 1975, concluded that 68% of the job losses were due to technological change, 17.2% to imports from other developed countries, and 14.8% to imports from poorer countries. The loss of jobs through technological change has to be accepted as inevitable, but job losses through increased imports from other developed countries, and through imports from developing countries deriving from British investment there, raise serious issues for international development.

The Multi-Fibre Arrangement (MFA) was designed in 1974 to control the level of imports into developed countries from the cheap labour countries of the Third World, and at the same time to allow Third World countries to benefit from the advantages of industrialisation and to make the most of their cheap labour. However, when the company owing and the industry in the Third World comes from the West, the policy seems to have made a mockery of itself. The full benefits of industrialisation will be denied to the Third World if the industrialisation takes place under Western control.

THE MADURA CONNECTION

In India in 1880, the embryo of what was later to become Madura Coats made its appearance. In that year, Andrew and Frank Harvey of Neilston, near Glasgow set up in Bellary, South India, as cotton agents, in an area noted for its cotton-growing.

They quickly hit on the idea of processing the cotton themselves, rather than just selling it to spinners. It took them only three years to set up a mill in the unlikely spot of Ambasamudram. As a town it is very small, remote from cities and markets and infamous for malaria.

However, the Harvey brothers' decision to build a mill there in 1883 was a wise one. The construction of a dam, in combination with a natural waterfall with a 300-foot head of water, provided the mill with its power. The same system, with modifictions, is still in action today.

Within ten years of the establishment of this first mill, A. and F. Harvey opened two further mills in Tamil Nadu State, at Tuticorin and Madura. Over the years the brothers expanded and developed their textile operations, producing cotton, blended yarn and industrial textiles. At the same time, the company established itself as a Managing Agent, acting for Madura Mills, another textile company, as well as pursuing other interests in shipping and insurance.

J. & P. COATS

Coats made its first appearance in India via thread exported from the U.K. in the 1880's. It was not until 1920 that the company's own selling organisation, the Central Agency, opened a branch in Bombay, subsequently opening further branches in Calcutta, Delhi and Madras.

In 1937 through a minor rewinding unit, Coats started up production in a small way in India. Not until 1953 was a full-scale mill complex opened at Koratti in Kerala. The plant produced high quality thread designed for sale in place of imported thread. This plant remained Coats' sole major production venture in India until 1974, when J. & P. Coats merged with A. & F. Harvey and Madura Mills.

The Emergence of Madura Coats

Coats Harvey and Madura Mills had been drawing closer together over the years through cross-shareholding, and the purchasing of one another's products. The newly merged company took the name of Madura Coats. J. & P. Coats was its principal shareholder, with 68% of the equity.

In 1973 the Indian government, in a round of policy-making aimed at bringing the economy under control, passed the Foreign Exchange Regulation Act (FERA). Through the Act the Government sought to introduce elementary control of foreign investment and multinationals by restricting all foreign investment holdings. Madura Coats was judged by the Government to be working in a non-priority area with respect to the country's development, and was requested to dilute its foreign equity holding to 40%. As a result, J. & P. Coats sold 28% of its shares to Indian nationals and Indian financial institutions, although it remained by far the largest single shareholder.

Today, Madura Coats is consolidating its production and market position as a leading thread and textile producer and seller. A clear decision has also been made to diversify from its traditional textile role. In 1979, it made a major investment in Hyderabad Electronics, a producer of medical equipment, and has applied for a production licence for Nylon-66 to be produced in a new plant in Andra Pradesh.

HOW MADURA COATS OPERATES

Objects

The company's objective is the manufacture of yarn, industrial textiles, cloth, cotton hank, handcraft thread, cotton and synthetic thread and other textile products.

Employment

Apart from one very small plant in the north all of Madura Coats 22,000 employees are based in the south of India. The breakdown is as follows:
Madurai (Tamil Nadu), 8,500 workers in thread, cloth and industrial textiles.
Ambasamdudram (Tamil Nadu), 6,000 workers in thread and cloth.
Koratti (Kerala), 3,000 workers in fixing and finishing thread.
Tuticorin (Tamil Nadu), 3,000 workers in spinning and thread production.
Bangalore and sales offices, 1,250 workers.

In sharp contrast to the U.K., where 85% of Coats workers are women, only 500 out of the 22,000 employees in India are women, and they are restricted to one work shift in Kerala and assorted office posts.

Products

By glancing at the production table listed below (p. 53) you will get a flavour of the range of goods produced by the company. They range from thread for kite-flying, to denims, to military contracts, to thread for export.

In 1979-80 total sales amounted to 1,206 million Rupees, that is £51 million. 88% of the sales are absorbed by the Indian market and 12% by the export market. Mr. P.G. Menon, the Madura Coats Personnel Manager estimated that Madura Coats had approximately 20% of the entire Indian thread market, and that thread production accounted for one third of the company's output.

Of the 12% of turnover exported, approximately 10% is made up of thread. The rest includes industrial textiles, cloth, and now finished clothes. The major sales areas are Bangladesh and Sri Lanka, where Coats have no production bases, the U.S.A., Europe, the U.K. and, to a lesser extent the Soviet Union and other countries. The export contracts to the U.S., Europe, the U.K., the Soviet Union and elsewhere are won through Coats Patons' international marketing network. At the minimum, a fee is paid by Madura Coats to Coats Patons for winning each sales contract. The Reserve Bank of India has given clearance for such fee paying.

WHO OWNS MADURA COATS?

Madura Coats has 4,800 equity shareholders. The ownership is however concentrated in the top ten shareholders, who in November 1979 laid claim to 8.5 million equity shares out of a total of 11.6 million. J. & P. Coats, with 40% of the total equity, has significant shareholding control. Not only has Coats more than four times the equity of the next major shareholder, it is also dealing with other major shareholders who are, so to speak, "sleeping"—their equity holding representing little more than an investment by nationalised insurance and unit trust companies.

Madura Coats is defined as an associate company of Coats Patons, and not as a subsidiary, as Coats Patons only owns a minority of the total shareholding. In the 1979 Annual Report, Coats Patons admits operating with a strong production and management relationship between H.Q. and the operation of associates. This is certainly true in the case of Madura Coats, where the flow of company information and decisions is reinforced by British top management, and a board of directors, four of the ten members of which are from the U.K.

Production & Sales

Madura Coats operations are split into four main groups

	Workers	Factories	Products	Sales
Thread Group	6500 (production & sales)	Koratti (production) & Tuticorin & Madurai.	Good quality cotton and synthetic thread, for use in products from kite-flying to umbrellas to shoes. Use Trade Mark of Chain. Anchor and Griffin.	See Commercial Group
Cloth Group	6200	Ambasamudram (1,199 looms)	Weaving cloth with ancillary processes of bleaching, dying and finishing. Denims, tussores, tioles, casements, shirtings, poplins, etc.; in cotton and synthetic. Suitings and Shirtings. Special use: ventile parachute fabric.	9.3 million metres exorted. 66.7m Rupees-worth exported. Largely U.K., U.S.A., with smaller amounts to U.S.S.R, West Germany, other countries.
Industrial Textile Group	7,000	Madurai, Serampore	Warp sheets used in tyre manufacture. Belting ducts used in conveyor and transmission belts. Canvas for industry and Indian military use. Also jeep and lorry covers. Filter cloth. Industrial yarns—used in making fan belts.	250 million Rupees inland. 40 million Rupees exported. U.S.A., U.S.S.R., U.K., Denmark, West Germany, Australia, New Zealand.
Commercial Group	1,500	Overall: to contribute to growth through exports, imports and trading.	Sells mill textiles made by other mills. Sells hand and power loom produce, nationally and for export. Markets dhotis, saris, sheets and towels. Supplies garments to large-volume chain stores in Italy, Germany, U.K. (non-boutique). Dye springs, product technology used in dyeing yarn.	Approximately 10% of total turnover is exported in the form of thread.

Coats Patons: A Scottish Company in India

In 1979-80, equity funds accounted for £107m and loan funds £57m. That is, for approximately every £2 of equity £1 was borrowed. In the same year total turnover amounted to £51.3 million, with a gross profit declared of £7.6 million. For the shareholders, it was a good year—to celebrate the centenary of the Harvey Brothers' first Indian operation, a special dividend of 20% was declared!

Madura Coats Management and Managers

It is only at the very top of the tree that Coats Patons managers are to be found. The positions they occupy are vital. The Madura Coats Board of Directors is as follows:

Chairman
Sir Muthia Chettiar (a member of one of South India's wealthiest families, with a large private shareholding in Madura Coats).

Managing Director
To 1981—Mr. M.B.S. Henry. From 1981—Mr. M.G. Pratt. (Both came from previous Coats Patons management jobs—Mr. Henry from Latin America, Mr. Pratt from the post of Manufacturing Director, J. & P. Coats Paisley).

Deputy Managing Director, Thread Group
Mr. H.T. Clifton (Manufacturing Manager, Coats Paton, Glasgow, 1970-80).

Directors
T.K. Raghavachari
Dr. M. Ramaswamy
C.S. Vidyasankar
N. Ramanand Roa
N.L. Kirby (a Briton, and General Manager of the Commercial Group)
S.K. Malhotra (full-time Director, and General Manager of Madurai Mills).
C.R. Thakore
M.B.S. Henry (retired Managing Director)

There is another Briton who is not a member of the Board of Directors, the fourth and final member of the expatriate top-management pool: Mr Colin Miller, Deputy General Manager and Weaving Manager, the Fifth Briton, apart from Messrs. Pratt, Clifton, Kirby and Miller, is Mr. Henry, who provides part-time services as a Board member.

All of the Britons are based at company H.Q. in Bangalore. Indian managers are in charge at plant level.

Coats Patons: A Scottish Company in India

In India, Madura Coats has its own Product Development section, and another concerned with Research and Development in cotton. However, when it comes to thread technology, and information regarding innovation and management, instructions come from Glasgow.

A joke circulates among Madura Coats managers. A competition is organised for the company's senior and middle managers. The first prize is one week in Glasgow, and the second is two weeks in Glasgow!

The list of the top ten Madura Coats Shareholders in November 1979.

Names of ten highest holders	Number of Shares
1. J. & P. Coats, Ltd.	4,641,296
2. Life Insurance Corporation of India	1,109,521
3. Unit Trust of India	986,451
4. United India Insurance Co. Ltd.	431,577
5. Mr. R. Ramanathan Chettiar	314,000
6. New India Assurance Co. Ltd.	305,089
7. Madura South India Corporation Pvt. Ltd.	260,160
8. Kidarnath Kishanchand Private Ltd.	246,424
9. National Insurance Co. Ltd.	132,955
10. Mr. R. Ramaswamy	118,000
TOTAL	8,545,473

WAGES AND CONDITIONS

Shop floor workers

Working from an exchange rate of 16 rupees to the £1 (the going rate in September 1981), the wages of shop-floor workers are as follows. On average an unskilled employee will receive £40 a month, a skilled worker £45 a month, and an overlooker £51 a month. A further group of workers, termed "trainees", and accounting for about one in ten of the workforce, are only paid £14.50 a month. The creation of "trainee" workers has been very contentious. In some ways it is like a Youth Opportunity Programme for adults that has been institutionalisted into the company rules. On joining the company, a worker is given trainee status for a minimum of two years before being confirmed as a permanent worker and put on the higher wage scale with paid holidays. As it is generally agreed that the jobs in Madura Coasts are at best of a semi-skilled nature and that workers are fully trained after three months, the resentment against this system shown by the workforce is hardly surprising.

The basic working week consists of 6 working days of eight hours each, on a revolving shift basis—one week day shift, next week back-shift, the third night-shift—before returning to the day shift and so on. No extra pay is given for shift work. The mills are kept open for 7 days a week and worked for 24 hours a day.

By the Factory Act, workers (apart from trainees) are entitled to 12-14 days paid holiday per year. This is calculated on the basis of one day's paid holiday per 20 working days. To be eligible for paid leave, an employee must work 240 days. On top of this, there is 9 days' paid leave for Festivals and National Holidays.

Both the company and the employees contribute to the State Insurance scheme which gives the worker entitlement, if certified ill, to 50% of pay for 90 days, and then nothing—it stops. The scheme also covers basic health treatment for the immediate family. On a wage of £45 per month the workers are considered beneath the tax threshold, but they are subjected to deductions for the Provident Fund and the union.

After deductions the average wage is approximately £40 per month. Is that a good or bad wage?

In comparison to the workers of Paisley, who do the same job on a 40-hour week basis and earn, at the top, about £320 a month, Madura Coats' employees are obviously poorly paid. But to assess the value of their wages in Indian terms is not easy. In comparison with other industrial plants in Madurai, Coats Patons was regarded as the third best employer, after a motor-bike company and an industrial textile concern. But in India, take home wages will generally have to support a household of at least six people—the worker and his wife, their children, and two or more elderly or unemployed relatives.

In comparison to the people who tend a flock of goats all day, or walk the streets selling ripe coconuts, the Madura Coats workers receive a decent income. But unlike the goat-herd, or the casual worker, Madura Coats employees are generally working on piece rate, for a wealthy Western-based company which can afford to declare a 20% dividend for its shareholders.

Management Wages

A qualified accountant will earn approximately £414 a month, about nine times the wage of a shop-floor worker. As one moves up again to Managing Director level, the wage rates take another leap. Officially the Managing Director receives £1,835 a month.

In the U.K. the gap between an apprentice and the boss of a company of Madura Coats' size will probably be in the order of 1 to 20—£3000 a year to £60,000. In Madura Coats the ratio is 1 to 126, with the trainee receiving £14.50 a month and the Managing Director £414 a month.

Working conditions

The textile industry in the United Kingdom itself had a bad health and safety record. The processes involved in textile manufacture present various problems: noise and deafness; toxic substances; dust from carding, spinning and weaving; chemicals from synthetic fibres and dyeing.

One of the most toxic dusts is that created in processing cotton—the raw material most used by Madura Coats. The production undertaken by Madura Coats subjects the workers to noise, toxic dust and chemicals as well as to contact with fast-moving machinery.

Madura Coats does not keep health and safety records and the company refused the author permission to inspect their factories. The lack of figures suggests that health problems are tucked away with other problems created for the community—except that after fifteen or twenty years the workers will pay the physical price. But from secondary evidence supplied by workers, trade union officials and medical personnel in the State Hospital, Madurai, it is clear that Madura Coats workers are especially liable to lung disease and the other diseases associated with textile production.

Perhaps the last word should be left to P.G. Menon, Madura Coats' Personnel Manager. When asked to compare the health and safety conditions in Madura Coats to conditions in European textile firms he replied: "Very poor".

THE TRADE UNIONS

The conventional role of trade unions is to represent the interests of the workers' relations with management, the trade unions providing a counter-vailing power to the power of the management. And that is just about acceptable to everyone—for who will disagree with the aphorism that power tends to corrupt?

If it were only the case that the more trade unions the workers have, the better their interests are represented, the workers of Madura Coats should surely be among the best treated in the world. There are no fewer than **46** unions representing the 22,000 Madura Coats workers in India. The major unions are split down political party/trade union lines, with each political party, of which there are many, having a corresponding union. The Congress Party has I.N.T.U.C. (Indian National Trade Union Congress), the Communist Party of India has A.I.T.U.C. (All-India Trade Union Congress), D.M.K., a Southern political movement, has a D.M.K. Union, the Communist Party (Marxist) has C.I.T.U. (Congress of Indian Trade Unions), and so the story continues, with the addition of unions representing the more professionalised/skilled sections of the workforce, and others formed to follow particular leaders.

The unions themselves compete for membership, and just to oblige, as well as to give themselves that extra union cover, some workers in Tamil Nadu belong to two, three or four unions.

To understand the union structure properly, one has to take account of two separate industrial relations systems. Firstly, there is Tamil Nadu, with 17,000 Madura Coats workers, and secondly, Koratti in Kerala, with a workforce of 3,000. In Kerala there are two main unions—a well-established "works" union, and an I.N.T.U.C. Union, with a few smaller unions representing sections of skilled workers. Here, the unions have a certain unity of purpose in representing and pressing for the workers' interests. An indication of the cohesion of the unions' organisation is that wages in Kerala are 10% higher than in Tamil Nadu. In Tamil Nadu, the unions compete, the management help perpetuate the divide, and corruption is commonplace.

Not surprisingly the workers have come to mistrust the unions. The brunt of the workers' charges in Ambasamudram and Madurai (which between them account for 14,000 workers) was borne by I.N.T.U.C. (the Congress union), D.M.K. (the union affiliated to the Southern popular party of the same name), and H.M.S. (Hind Mazdoor Sabha—a union with some quasi-socialist leanings).

The charge brought against these unions was that they agreed too readily to management wishes. This did not surprise the workers, since they knew that the officials of these unions were corrupt. If the union officials sought to represent anyone's interests, it was their own—and the management were only too happy to oblige by materially providing for them, in return for the *quid pro quo* of easy settlements.

Many workers had tales of petty forms of collaboration between management and union officials. Many of these can possibly be dismissed, but a core of evidence remains which suggests that these three unions are no more than an extension of Madura Coats' industrial relations wing.

In May 1978, a state-level strike started in Tamil Nadu. Thirty days after it started, INTUC, DMK, ADMK, and HMS unions in Madura Coats at Madurai broke the strike, and called on their members to return to work. The members did not comply; they defied the return-to-work call and stayed out with the other unions. After another 24 days the strike was resolved, and the workers received a wage increase of 45 R's (£2.70) and an extra 2 days' paid holiday a year.

58

INTUC, DMK, and HMS are known to have good relations with the management. This means that workers tend to join these unions in the way that people in the U.K. take out an insurance policy. You don't need to believe in the union—the only reason you join is to get them to fight your case if a petty dispute breaks out over piece-rate, time-keeping, keeping at the job, and so on. Some workers joined the above unions because they followed the politics of their political party. For others the reverse was the case—membership was used as a camouflage for opposing political views. You may be victimised if you belong to particular unions, most notably CITU, the union of the Communist Party (Marxist).

If you belong to CITU as a trainee, you can expect to be a trainee for a good bit longer than the normal two years. And, much worse, as a CITU member you would almost definitely be deprived of your right to "introduce an heir"—a scheme whereby a worker with 15 years' service can introduce a close relative to the company for employment. And in an area where jobs are incredibly scarce, that is a major factor in deciding on your choice of union.

A measure of the trust which workers place in some unions, and of their distrust of others, can be gathered from the results of elections of office-bearers to run the Madura Coats Credit Society (Retailing) in Ambasamudra. In both instances all six office-bearers were CITU members. It was suggested—perhaps by a partisan source—that this demonstrated that the workers trusted CITU members with money, unlike representatives of other unions. I am not familiar with the political composition of the co-operative societies in Madurai, and cannot therefore judge how much trust is placed in CITU members there. I do not want to suggest glibly that CITU is beyond reproach, but it did seem that Madura Coats workers felt more respect for CITU than for the other unions. Despite the strong disincentives to joining CITU, in Ambasamudram it has the support of 700 of the 5,000 workers.

The most depressing example of corruption among workers' represent-atives is in the area of recruitment policy. Traditionally recruitment has been based on the right of an heir—or close family member—to be introduced to employment after 15 years service. In the past few years this had changed with workers coming into employment "under the counter".

At the annual management-union negotiation sessions on workers' conditions, it has become standard practice for management to present union officials from DMK, INTUC and HMS with a number of jobs for their personal distribution. In turn, the union officials sell these jobs to potential employees at a going rate, today, of about 10,000-12,000 R's each-the equivalent of the first three years' wages. The money raised in this way provides a nice perk for the officials concerned, and one can only speculate on how it might effect negotiations with management. The company personnel manager estimated that of every 100 recruits, about 40 or 50 had purchased their jobs in some way.

In Koratti, the story is altogether different. The workers are represented by two unions, the Jaman Thread Mills Labour Union—an independent union with support right across the political spectrum, and a membership of 1,500—and Madura Coats Workers' Union, which has 600 members, and is affiliated to the Congress (I) Party. These two work together surprisingly well, in the light of the goings-on in Tamil Nadu, and actually go so far as to co-operate with the staff union, which is also independent of political affiliations. The Jaman Thread Mills Union was really an unparalleled revelation—the Secretary belonged to an extreme left-wing party, the President was a member of the right-wing Janata, and the membership embraced all sorts of political creeds.

Koratti works on the basis of a 3-4 year agreement with the management. There is generally industrial peace for the duration of the agreement, and mayhem at negotiation time. The last time, in 1978, **the strike lasted four months.** The Keralites have a reputation for industrial militancy— deservedly, when you consider what it means to have no income for your family for four consecutive months. In the course of my visit, I found that the resources of the credit and retail co-ops for lending were heavily called upon, and that families got by by going into debt and selling jewellery.

Management and Workers

India is a country of the poor and the rich, with very little in between. In reviewing the respective wage rates of workers and the salaries plus perks of the managers, one sees just how well Madura Coats takes advantage of and reinforces the pattern.

As was pointed out earlier the earnings gap between the top man and the trainees was 126 to 1. However, the dual standards do not stop there. As Mr. Menon explained "we have to do certain things" to keep salary levels up in the face of a progressive personal tax structure and maximum wage regulations.

One of these "things" seems to be straight-forward handouts from the company's "black money" account, the existence of which is an open secret. The second major "thing" is a bit more sophisticated.

At each production centre—Madurai, Ambasamudram, Tuticorin and Koratti—special compounds are created and reserved for the upper management. These compounds are walled off—all entry is limited, and checked by Madura Coats security men. Inside, there are rows of attractive bungalows, with gardens and air-conditioning and, among other facilities, a shared swimming-pool. Normally, this is the only swimming pool in town. Each house is served by its small quota of domestics—two, three or four servants (possibly more), and a company car with chauffeur. An allocation for house rent and servants' wages is deducted from the individual manager's basic salary, but this can be paid back to the manager through a a tax loop, since the expenses incurred are classified as "maintaining the property of the company"—in this case, the superior housing estate of Madura Coats.

Only a limited salary boost can be given through expenses, since by law expenses cannot exceed one-third of salary. Mr. M.B.S. Henry, the previous Managing Director, had a reputation for "lavish" management style and living, and was reputed to have 39 servants at his modest Bangalore abode.

The privileged life-style of Madura Coats' top management only reflects the culture of India itself—a good life for those hailing from good families. But Madura Coats shows little regard for Indian values in the provision it makes for its workers. There is strong paternalistic strain in Indian society; managers are expected to look after their workers, and to make provision for housing, clothing for work, and food during the work period. Madura Coats supplies little housing, and no food or clothing. The only example of housing provided by the company for ordinary employees is in Madurai, where there is a "workers colony" of approximately 90 houses. These houses, though cheap, are none too pleasant, with no running water, gas or electricity, and a drainage channel running between the rows of dwellings. The houses are back to back and side by side, with only a very small window at the front, and barely enough room for all six inhabitants to sleep under cover during the monsoon.

So while Madura Coats offers the Indian manager, invariably of good family, a chance to acquire Western ways and wealth, it keeps its workers firmly within the severe restrictions of an "ordinary" Indian standard of living.

Multinational versus home product

As an affiliate of a major multinational company Madura Coats intrudes the powerful forces of international capitalism and technological production into an underdeveloped, and hence fragile social and economic system. Certainly the company provides 22,000 jobs at wages above the Indian average. But those jobs are bought at a high price in terms of the destruction of the traditional jobs and way of life of hundreds of thousands if not millions of people.

The International Labour Office (I.L.O.) carried out two studies on living conditions in India in the years 1963-64 and 1973-74, and compared their findings after ten years.

In 1963-64, 40.2% of the people lived below the absolute poverty level of 1,935 calories a day, and 5.2% of people lived below the extraordinary poverty level of 1,720 calories a day. By 1973-74, 78.5% of the people were living below the poverty level of 1,935 calories a day, and 42% of the people below the extraordinary level of 1,720 calories a day.

In 1973, when the population was 650 million (approx.), about 510 million were living below the poverty line. Today, the population is 700 million, and the number of people living below the poverty line in India is greater than the whole population of Europe. At the same time, one has to recognise that the top 20% of the population have experienced an improvement in their material living conditions.

After food, as a basic need, come clothes and housing. Clothing is, of course, the area of production with which Madura Coats is concerned. Mahatma Gandhi made the case of the Indian peasant clear to the world: the basic needs of the peasant man, woman and family were to grow their own food, prepare their own primitive thread and work it into cloth on their handloom, and organise their own sanitary system. These simple life-lines were fragile, and needed careful tending.

The distribution of population between country and town has not changed substantially. For hundreds of millions of Indians, the level of consumption remains minimal, and what they consume is obtained through their own hard graft in the fields, growing crops and tending animals, and through their long and tedious efforts spinning thread and making material on their hand and power looms.

The machinery needed to spin one's own thread and to handloom cloth for sale is very simple. Most of the labour required to produce the finished product comes from the worker rather than from the machines. Imagine, however, the conflict of interest between the domestic handloom weaver and the Madura Coats worker: the one perhaps spends the first hours of the day in his yard, spinning his thread, and then the rest of the day sitting cross-legged on a floor, powering his hand loom with his own energy and supervising all its different functions; the other tends a Madura Coats tube-winder with 2,800 rotations a minute, and will produce, in an eight hour shift, 240 dozen tubes of finished thread, which then pass on to the automatic weaving division to be turned into great lengths of cloth.

The battle between the primitive producer and the automated company, with its national promotion, product development and sales is hardly a battle at all. It plainly and overwhelmingly amounts to decimation of the small producer—whose loom often constitutes his family's access to any kind of income.

The primitive producer just can't compete on an equal footing with the big-time automated factories; his product is comparatively expensive for its quality, his marketing is minimal, his outlets restricted, and his product development nil.

The Government of India has introduced various pieces of legislation in an attempt to protect the primitive textile producer by restricting the licences issued to mass-production automatic plants. Such moves have been limited, and have not halted the logical marketing and mechanical developments unleashed by the introduction of mechanised processes.

Madura Coats is not the only advanced textile company in India, nor did it deliberately set out to impoverish the vast network of primitive producers. However, the effect of its operation has been to impoverish this sector, and to obsorb, bit by bit, small surpluses that these producers gained through their sales.

FINANCE AND PROFIT

It is often argued—and has been argued specifically in the case of Coats Patons—that a multinational company entering a Third World market introduces fresh capital. It should, however, be noted that 33% (£57.2 million) of Madura Coats' capital assets in 1979-80 were in the form of loans raised in India at the prevailing, relatively cheap, rate. These loans helped to secure the 20% dividend for equity shareholders from which J. & P. Coats benefitted, with 7% dividends for preference shareholders and 7¾% for debenture shareholders.

A second major point in connection with finance concerns the repatriation of profits.

In 1979-80 the company agreed on a 15% for Equity shareholders, plus a special 5% Centenary Dividend. In other words, a dividend of 20% on Equity shares. That means that for each Equity share with a face value of 10 Rupees, a dividend of 2 Rupees will be paid. Coats Paton has 4,641, 296 Equity shares at 10 Rupees' face value (a total value of 46,412,960 R's), and consequently received 9,282,592 R's as its share of Madura Coats dividend (£546,034 at 17 R's to the £).

P.G. Menon forwarded to me figures from the company's Finance Manager which state repatriated profit from Madura Coats to Coats Patons in 1979-80 as being 6,900,000 Rupees, plus a further 200,000 R's in commission for sales contracts won by Coats Patons sales teams, bringing the total repatriated sum to 7,100,000 R's (£417,647 at 17 R's to the £). That means that "officially", Coats Paton repatriated £417,647 from India to the U.K. in 1980. What the actual figure is remains a matter for speculation—the company does not make public the extent to which Coats Patons benefits from transfer pricing and tax avoidance.

TAX

It is often pointed out that one of the main ways in which a multinational firm contributes to the local economy is through the payment of taxes into the national coffers. In 1979-80, Madura Coats paid tax on its profit of 43.5 million Rupees, approx £2.2 million, as well as revenue provided by the personal tax paid by its better renumerated staff.

But more significant than local tax manoeuvres is Coats Patrons' use of the flexibility it enjoys as a multinational company. On information supplied by a contact with several years' experience in Madura Coats, headquarters division, it is possible to reconstruct how Coats Patons uses its international network to reduce its tax liability, using the process known as "transfer pricing".

1. Coats Patons through its sales agent, wins a contract for thread in Egypt.
2. India is contacted and asked to fulfil this contract. When the work is finished, the thread is shipped directly to Egypt.
3. Egypt receives the thread, and pays the fee for its delivery to Coats Patons (Glasgow).
4. Coats Patons (Glasgow) retains part of that fee, and pays costs, plus perhaps a bit extra, to Madura Coats.
5. Madura Coats then pays the straightforward fee to Coats Patons for winning the contract, and retains the rest as its own sales income.

The critical point is at stage 4., where what is known as "transfer pricing" may be taking place. If at this stage Coats Patons holds back income which should have legitimately gone to India and instead declares it in its tax returns in the U.K., the company will have benefitted from being taxed at the British rate of taxation which is lower than in India. In consequence tax benefits to India are reduced.

'STRIP AND BURN'

In 1980, Oxfam spent one-tenth of its entire budget in India, which is a priority area for expenditure. That sum equalled £981,059. But Madura Coats alone sends back to the U.K. every year half of what Oxfam is able to send to India—and that is without taking into account the discrepancy between official figures on repatriated profits, and the actual sums finding their way back to the parent company. Nor does it begin to reflect the activities of all the other companies which repatriate profits from India to Britain.

Coats Patons: A Scottish Company in India

It is argued that Coats Patons have created this surplus in India, and it is therefore their right to remove part of it. Two contrary claims deserve consideration. First, these profits have in large been generated by the long hours, hard work and low rates of pay of thousands of Indian workers, who are, in effect, doing an "Oxfam shop" in reverse, producing surpluses which are sent back to the U.K. Secondly, Coats has taken over a market on which indigenous labour-intensive producers were dependent, and into which they might have expanded, had not large companies like Coats Patons simply squeezed them out.

All in all, it is difficult to avoid the conclusion that the Coats Patons empire is interested only in securing its own objectives, regardless of whether its interests conflict with those of the communities within which it operates. At one time, there was a system called "strip and burn" farming. Today, it seems, it's "strip and burn" business.

THE MULTINATIONAL PHENOMENON

Alan Sinclair

When Wiggins Teape, a subsidiary of British American Tobacco, Britain's third largest company announced in May 1980 that it was to close its paper mill at Corpach, near Fort William with the loss of 400 jobs, the decision was denounced as a modern version of the Highland Clearances.

There is indeed a rough parallel between Lord Lovat, the Duke of Argyll and Lady Matheson on the one hand and International Business Machines, Coats Patons and British American Tobacco on the other. As landowners could once dispossess hundreds or in some cases thousands of tenants, today giant companies can deprive hundreds of employees of the jobs which are their means of livelihood and the source of their social status. In each case the pattern of ownership and management determines the way income and wealth is distributed, as well as the location of jobs and the economic health of the community as a whole. Like the landowners the multinational companies act as society's planners.

Already in Scotland three out of every five jobs in manufacturing industry are in companies controlled from outwith Scotland, many of them multinationals. Foreign multinationals created 104,00 manufacturing jobs in Scotland between 1954 and 1974, 54% of the total. Over the period the foreign multinationals' contribution to new manufacturing jobs grew from 53% in 1954-1959 to 74% in 1969-74.

The continued concentration of industry and the introduction of new technologies which, according to some estimates, will cut the manufacturing labour requirement by nine-tenths by the year 2000, point to an ever more dominant role for the multinationals, the implications of which challenge the limits of present day political and economic thinking.

With significant proportions of investment, production and employment already controlled by multinationals, there is a need for their operations to be opened up for scrutiny and debate. Working from the dictum that if one wants to understand the poor, one should study the rich, it could be said that in order to understand de-industrialisation, the Scottish experience—or zero industrialisation, the experience of much of the Third World—one should study the multinational companies. And to understand the role of MNC's in Scotland and in the Third World we obliged, by the pattern of operations of the companies themselves, to look at the international perspective.

The Growing Season of MNC's

MNC's have come of age. General Motors, the world's largest company (trading in Britain mainly as Vauxhall, Opel and Bedford), produces one in three of all cars and trucks sold in the West, and has plants in 127 countries. James Finlay and Company of Glasgow, one of the few survivors of Scotland's commercial expansion in the 18th century, is today among Scotland's top twenty companies, with plantations in Kenya, India and Bangladesh, and interests in energy, insurance and property. Like General Motors and Finlay's, all MNC's operate on an international scale, and obey a rigorous financial logic. That logic was succinctly expressed by *Business International,* the voice of the multinational business community, in 1967.

> "The global company views the world as a single entity. Its perspectives transcend all national boundaries. Decisions are made not in terms of what is best for the home country or any particular product group, but in terms of what is best for the corporation as a whole on an international basis . . . Taking the whole world as their market, they tend to organise production, distribution and selling activities with as little regard for national (political) boundaries as the realities of time and space permit."

The term "multinational" covers a variety of forms of international business enterprises. Their lowest common denominator is that they have business operations in more than one country, but the typical multinational is distinguished by the fact that it has operations in several countries, by its large size in terms of turnover and labour force, and by the maintenance of financial control by company headquarters.

The ancestors of today's MNC's were the trading and shipping companies founded in the formative years of the British Empire. The British Imperial East Africa Company, the British India Company and the Hudson Bay Company thrived in the days before strong interventionist government, although some, like the East India Company, depended on Royal Charter. However, a number of political and technological factors peculiar to this century have propelled MNC's to their position of pre-eminence.

Firstly, there was the sustained growth produced by the post-Keynesian political consensus in the West. Demand management—the manipulation of public expenditure through capital spending programmes, and of private sector demand through redistributive and fiscal controls—enabled governments throughout the developed world to maintain rates of economic growth between 1945 and the early 1970's which were exceptional by historical standards. Secondly, alongside a buoyant domestic market, the world monetary order constructed at Bretton Woods at the close of World War II meant that trading conditions for Western industrialised countries were good. Thirdly, these factors have operated in an era of continuing technological advance, embracing the internal combustion engine, mass production, synthetic substitutes, cheap energy supplies, the computer, telecommunications, and now the micro-chip.

These conditions have allowed MNC's to capitalise on their three major advantages—finance, technology and marketing. For an MNC, finance is readily available: they have abundant collateral, they are attractive propositions for local investment funds, they can transfer resources from profit centres to initiate or support operations elsewhere, and they have developed the closest personal and institutional links with the international banks. In an age of high technology, the costs to a newcomer of challenging multinational dominance are high, and the prospects of success poor. The research, design and tooling-up costs involved in developing new technology are prohibitive, quite apart from the structures of patent law. Marketing costs and the projection of a "product image", the creation of a distribution network and the provision of an after-sales service, also impose high costs on new entrants to the market. Each of these factors gives MNC's an advantage over national competitors. When combined as elements of a company's world-wide strategy, they enhance and reinforce MNC control of the processes of production and distribution, and enable them to achieve market dominance.

Multinationals at Large: the Dimensions of Multinational Operations

The consequence of the evolution of companies able to take advantage of the new international economic buoyancy has been to transform the basic structure of the economy, nationally and internationally. In the 1979 General Election in Britain, the Finchley family butcher was held up as a paradigm of enterprise and service to the community; but although small may be beautiful, the facts tell us quite clearly that today, "big is where it's at".

By the early 1970's, MNC's, with a growth rate about twice that of the non-multinational sector, were producing about a fifth of the world G.N.P., excluding centrally planned economies. International production by MNC's in non-Communist nations exceeded the aggregate exports of other companies in such countries.[2]. In 1973 the sales of General Motors were bigger than the G.N.P. of Switzerland, Pakistan or South Africa, while the sales of Royal Dutch Shell exceeded the G.N.P.'s of Iran, Venezuela and Turkey.[3].

Within particular product markets, different MNC's hold ascendancy. International Business Machines (IBM) supplies 40% of the world computer market. Kodak supplies 90% of the British colour film market. Nestles, Lyons and General Foods (Maxwell House) sell between them 95% of all the coffee consumed in Britain. It becomes clear just how pervasive the influence of an MNC can be when we consider the number of products and lines marketed by a company like Unilever: Lux, Persil, Omo, Radiant, Astral, Pears, Surf, Sunlight, Sure, Squeezy, Vim, Sunsilk, Gibbs, Close-Up, Domestos, Blue Band, Stork, Summer County, Imperial, Echo, Spry, Crisp'n'Dry, Cookeen, Batchelors, Birds Eye, Walls, Unox, Vesta,

Cuppa Soup and John West. Not only do they market the above goods through chain stores and small shops throughout Britain, they also have their own retail outlets—Mattesons, MacFisheries and Liptons. And, if that's not mind-boggling enough, when you are away from Britain you can rely on picking up Unilever products in America, Africa, Australia and Asia.

Today, all the major factors in national and international economic activity—trade, prices, investment, employment and monetary policy—are significantly influenced by MNC activity. The volume and pattern of trade has changed, with many MNC's setting up production plants in countries which have previously only been export markets. Today, British-owned firms produce twice as much abroad as they actually export from the U.K., and 30% of all the world's trade is internal trading between different branches of one MNC. The increased concentration of production in MNC's also means that countries come to depend economically on the activities of a limited number of companies. In Britain, the top 100 companies account for half of the manufacturing output, assets and employment—and in consequence for half of the prices set in that sector. Internationally, in 1976 total investment amounted to $200 billion, half of which was controlled by 200 companies.

With respect to monetary policy, the 1976 Council of Europe *Report on Multinational Corporations* estimated that the MNC's have some $270 billion in liquid assets—more than twice the total reserves of all the world's central banks and international financial institutions put together. Such pools of liquidity give MNC's the opportunity to switch vast sums of "hot" money from currency to currency, to take advantage of movements in the speculative international money markets. The repatriation of profits by MNC's, and the drain on currency of loan repayment, can cause severe balance of payments problems, especially to Third World countries.

In theory, because MNC's have few competitors, they are not subjected to price competition. In practice, instances of gross over-pricing by MNC's have raised serious questions about the prices which they can and do charge. One of the most clearly-documented instances involved the price of Librium and Valium, tranquillisers produced by Hoffman-La Roche. In Italy, the prices paid for these drugs by the company subsidiary were £9 and £20 per kilo respectively; the British subsidiary had to pay £370 and £922 per kilo. After investigation in 1973 by the U.K. Monopolies Commission, Hoffman-La Roche were forced to lower these prices by 60% in the case of Librium, and by 75% in the case of Valium.

In economic theory and in popular politics, the company is supposed to be subordinate to the market, and the government sovereign over the nation. In practice, things are rather different. The concentration of market power in

69

The Multinational Phenomenon

the hands of a relatively small number of companies—the emergence of oligopoly—reduces the competitive impact of the market. Meanwhile governments are either reluctant to act, or find that their initiatives are defeated by the superior manoeuverability of the multinationals.

The Benefits of Multinational Companies

The costs and benefits of MNC operations cannot be tabulated in a straightforward book-keeping exercise. The Cambridge economist Joan Robinson suggests that there is only one thing worse than being exploited by a multinational, and that is **not** being exploited by a multinational. Some, like Jacques Maisonrouge, the publicity conscious European Director of IBM, offer a less paradoxical defence of the multinationals.

The U.S. owned I.B.M. is one of Europe's leading employers, providing 100,000 jobs, and producing from this base 90% of the goods it sells in Europe. In addition, IBM Europe purchases $1 billion plus of goods each year from 46,000 local suppliers. In Europe, it also develops its own products, employing 5,000 highly skilled people in its research laboratory and in its five development laboratories. Maisônrouge caps his case with the claim that if IBM had not produced and sold its goods in Europe, then the same goods would simply have had to be imported from the U.S.

Since MNC's hold such a considerable share of world commerce, production and investment, a country which has neither its own nor foreign MNC's working within its boundaries will have the greatest difficulty in achieving industrialisation. MNC's harness investment which creates employment through the building and staffing of plant. They stimulate the local economy through wages, and through the buying of goods and services for use in production. Central government gains the corporation and personal tax levied, and the economy as a whole benefits from the foreign exchange earned through exports. Finally, in addition to wages, the work force gains skill and experience which can be of future benefit in expanding production, and the consumer gains from the availability of a wider range of mass-produced goods. By enriching themselves, MNC's also enrich the communites within which they operate.

The Costs of Multinational Production

Adam Smith, the theoretical father of the free market, warned that capitalists are "forever trying to widen the market and narrow the competition . . . By raising profits above what they naturally would be, the (capitalists) levy for their own benefit an absurd tax on the rest of their fellow-citizens". In Smith's view, the capitalist was to be prevented from reaping excessive profits by the eagle eyes of other capitalists, who would be only too willing to move in and take a share of the profits. Today, when

MNC's have so many market advantages, and when, in a whole range of products from motor cars to margarine and gin, three or four companies supply 80-95% of U.K. sales, it is not difficult to argue that the regulatory mechanisms of the free market are no longer effective.

While MNC's do invest large amounts of capital, a look behind the company logo answers the question as to how MNC's come by their finance. In the first instance, MNC's attract investment and borrowing from local financial markets, through banks, insurance companies, and individual shareholders, and in subsequent cycles of investment, use is made of locally generated profits. In 1966, Frederick G. Donner, Chairman of General Motors, reflected on his own company's expansion overseas. His words are equally applicable to the company's subsequent record, and to that of other MNC's:

> "Let me summarise our overseas record during the last 15 years in terms of some objective measures of business accomplishments. At the end of 1950, the value of General Motors' net working capital and fixed overseas assets was about $180 million . . . By the end of 1965, this investment had increased to about $1.1 billion, or approximately six times the 1950 figure. This expansion was accomplished almost entirely from financial resources generated by General Motors operations abroad, and through local borrowings which could be repaid from local earnings. As a result . . . our overseas subsidiaries remitted about two-thirds of their earnings to the United States."

U.S. Department of Commerce figures show that in 1977 U.S. direct investment capital outflow to developing countries totalled $4,378 million, of which Latin America accounted for $3,999 million. However, U.S. companies' direct investment income from their Third World operations in the same year was $7,685 million, a net flow from the developing countries of $3,307 million.[4] Within this total, there was a small net capital flow from the U.S. to Latin America of $287 million, but this was more than offset by net flows to the United States from Central America, Africa, Asia, and, of course, from oil-producing countries of the Middle East.

Between 1970 and 1978 the value of U.S. investment in developing countries increased from $19 billion to $47 billion, but the annual income generated increased at twice the rate, from just under $3 billion to just under $9 billion. By comparison a total U.S. investment in **developed** countries of $137 billion million yielded income of $24 billion.[5] The general investment pattern is therefore one whereby MNC's harness existing investment surpluses in the host country, and in the second phase remove or reinvest the new surplus created.

With respect to employment, there is no guarantee that MNC investment will result in a net increase in jobs available. The evidence is conflicting, but there is a suggestion that when MNC's move into traditional industries, such as the soap industry in Kenya or the fruit drink industry in Nigeria, jobs are lost overall because of the technologically sophisticated and capital-intensive nature of MNC production. In the modern industries in Scotland where foreign MNC's tend to be concentrated, it is true that investment from a new electronics or car firm will result in an increase in the number of jobs available, but this in turn poses further questions: for example, why domestic industry, either private or public, has not taken advantage of this business opportunity, and whether there is a level of dependence on external capital which itself acts as an obstacle to the generation of local enterprise?

It cannot be argued in MNC's favour that they contribute substantially to government income through corporation tax. A report produced by *The Economist's* Intelligence Unit in 1981 revealed that major companies generally paid zero or marginal taxes.[6]. Through government incentives, the discounting of capital invested for tax purposes, and the shrewdness of the accountants operating the MNC's international structure, MNC's retain a significantly higher proportion of revenue than smaller firms. By using a technique called transfer pricing, MNC's manipulate the prices at which their subsidiaries in various countries buy and sell from one another, and can move the centre of profits of the whole enterprise to countries where taxes are lowest, and the laws most liberal.

One of the most serious problems associated with MNC's, and one not readily reduced to statistics, is their effect on the quality of life. To begin with, MNC operations increase inequality; only limited numbers of employees and investors actually benefit. MNC's cannot provide any solutions for Scotland, where one in five of the population lives in relative poverty, or for the Third World, where 40% of the population live in absolute poverty. The basic aim of MNC's is to sell their products and make surpluses, and in achieving this they respond to short-term cues given by individuals and communities who already possess purchasing power. It is not in the individual corporations' interest to support a fairer distribution of income, to look after the old or maintain employment levels.

Secondly, as you look around the modern world, you may want to reflect on the quality of the culture which MNC's have created. From Pot Noodles to identical, shiny green apples tasting either of petroleum or pulp; from newspapers controlled by oil conglomerates and cars built to disintegrate, to the insidious and seductive messages about personal satisfaction and social status which are part of each advertising campaign, MNC's are omnipresent. It is worth dwelling on the impact which MNC products, ideas and images make on our daily lives. Reflection on the products we consume will bring the point home more clearly than following up a dozen library references. The shaping of consumers' needs to match the future plans of MNC's is now squarely recognised by the British Institute of Marketing, who have changed their definition of marketing from "assessing consumer needs" to "assessing and converting consumer purchasing power into effective demand for a specific product . . . so as to achieve the profit target or other objectives set out by the company."[7]

Baby milk promotion in the Third World provides what is possibly the most vivid example of the pernicious effects which MNC marketing policy can have, even within one product range.

A number of MNC's promote dried baby milk in the Third World. Using product images which are usually of big, bouncing, white babies (although sometimes of the equivalent black super-babe), they market their product through thousands of outlets in Third World countries which have not positively legislated against its use, often providing free samples of milk to the new-born through the health services. This is particularly effective as a method of promotion, since after four or five days of bottle-feeding, it is unlikely that the mother will be able to resume breast-feeding successfully. The milk is expensive, and uses up huge proportions of the incomes of poor families; this in turn tempts the mother to over-dilute it. Artificial feeding is in any case unsuitable to the difficult environmental circumstances of most Third World mothers, who lack access to clean water and sterilisation facilities; and artificial milk does not protect the child against diarrhoea and disease to the same extent as breast milk.

The West has advocated and supported family planning programmes in the Third World for decades, and yet it is estimated that the effect of all these family planning programmes has been more than offset by the increase in artificial feeding in the Third World, which has robbed mothers of the natural period of reduced fertility during breast-feeding. The World Health Organisation, which should be able to defend the Third World against such practices, can only stand and stare: its entire annual budget is smaller than the advertising budget of Nestlés, one of the major companies involved.

In marketing and manufacturing their products, MNC's pursue policies which fit in with company plans and objectives. It is fortunate when the companies' interests happen to coincide with those of the community within which they operate. But how often is that the case? And what happens when the two sets of interests diverge?

How does Scotland fit in to the MNC pattern?

Scotland's relationships with multinational companies fall into four groups: (i) MNC's which are owned and registered in Scotland; (ii) MNC's operating in Scotland and controlled from elsewhere, including MNC's controlled from other parts of the U.K., the U.S.A., Europe, and the rest of the world; (iii) Scottish capital invested in MNC's operating overseas; (iv)

MNC goods consumed by Scottish industry, services and public.

(i) Scottish MNC's

Although in world terms Scottish MNC's are not in the super league, they do act nationally as major employers, investors and retailers. Table 1 sets out ten leading Scottish MNC's, giving names, placings in *The Times* top thousand British companies for 1980, main products, number of employees, and selected details indicating international operations. Two Scottish companies which should be included in the table in terms of size (Scottish and Newcastle Breweries and the House of Fraser) are excluded, as their operations are mainly concentrated in the domestic retail and jobs market. (See Table 1, page 79).

Scotland's major companies are highly integrated into the international market. Distillers' has 60% of turnover coming from sales outside the U.K., and Coats Patons employs 44,000 of its 65,000 workers overseas. But at the same time, as the table shows, the operations of Scotland's leading companies are relatively small, even in British terms: Low and Bonar and James Finlay are both well within the top 20 Scottish companies, and yet they rank 284 and 433 respectively in the top 1,000 British companies.

Working from figures produced by the Scottish Council Research Institute, it can be seen that during the 1970's, manufacturing employment declined more rapidly in Scottish-owned industries. In 1973, Scottish companies accounted for 44% of manufacturing employment; by 1979 it had fallen to 40%. (see Table II and III). This disproportionate decline in employment in Scottish owned manufacturing industries is in line with the concentration of such companies in the traditional sectors of food, mechanical engineering, textiles and timber.

(ii) Externally controlled MNC's in Scotland

This category includes two groups of companies. The first consists of companies based elsewhere in the U.K. with branches in Scotland— MNC's, nationalised industries with headquarters outside Scotland, and other smaller U.K. companies with headquarters outside Scotland. In total, non-Scottish U.K. companies with plants in Scotland accounted for a steady 39% of the manufacturing labour force throughout the 1970's—largely because of the role of the nationalised industries, which are major employers in shipbuilding, oil-refining, and the metal and coal industries.

The second group of companies consists of MNC's controlled outside the U.K., the majority based in North America, a few in Europe. In total, this group employs 109,000 people, 21% of Scotland's manufacturing workers, and is concentrated in the more dynamic modern sectors of instrument

74

engineering and electrical engineering. It includes many famous names, such as Burroughs, IBM, Playtex and Polaroid. Few economic sectors escape foreign penetration: even the whisky industry, Scotland's pride, has 24% of its workers employed by North American companies.

(iii) Scottish External Investment

Through banks, investment trusts, manufacturing companies, insurance and assurance companies, pension funds and private shares, money that is managed in Scotland at one turn is used at the next for acquiring foreign assets and shares.

The three main "Scottish" banks—the Clydesdale (wholly owned by the Midland Bank), the Bank of Scotland (35% owned by Barclays and 5.8% by the Kuwait Investment Office) and the Royal Bank (subject to competing take-over bids at the time of writing), between them held in March 1981 the sterling equivalent of £1,689 million in foreign assets, out of total assets of £8,106 million.

Scottish-based investment trusts, many of which were formed with the explicit aim of investing overseas, control between them £2,448 million, of which £909 million is invested overseas.

The total stock of foreign assets of Scottish-based banks and investment trusts is £2,598 million. To build up a complete picture of Scottish investment overseas, however, one would need to include the overseas investment of companies like Coats Patons, Low & Bonar and James Finlay, as well as the shares and assets held by insurance and assurance companies, pension funds and private individuals. The final figure would be a daunting one, especially when compared to the reverse flow here of the stock of foreign investment in Scotland.

In 1978, the Scottish Council (Development and Industry) calculated that the stock of manufacturing assets held by U.S. companies in Scotland was £650 million, with a further £12 million held by European companies. This total stock of foreign manufacturing assets worth £778 million would be slightly increased if one took into consideration three small Canadian-owned, and three small Japanese-owned plants. Although these assets are controlled by foreign MNC's, it is more than likely that the bulk of the funds involved was raised on the U.K. financial market, through the re-investment of returns made in an earlier period, or the use of government and regional incentives. The United States manufacturing assets are dwarfed by her oil interests in the United Kingdom. Some two-thirds of recoverable reserves, worth £270,000m. at current prices, are believed to be owned by U.S. companies.

The figure of £778 million of foreign manufacturing assets is still a minor one when compared to Scottish company investment abroad; Coats Patons alone reported overseas assets of £268 million in 1979, and the total of foreign financial assets held by banks, pension funds, investment trusts and private investors is significantly greater than the stock of foreign assets in Scotland excluding oil. In a period when the drying-up of domestic investment is recognised as one of our major economic problems, and when government policy is largely concerned with attracting foreign investment to Scotland, it is ironic that there should be so heavy a flow of investment from Scotland to overseas destinations. For Britain as a whole, nearly £13 billion has flowed overseas since the removal of exchange controls in 1979.

HOW THE THIRD WORLD FITS INTO THE MNC PATTERN

One quarter of all MNC investment is in the Third World. Third World countries are acutely aware of the need to industrialise, and see in the MNC's the answers to their own weak financial and industrial base.

Approximately 60% of the Third World's export earnings come from the export of primary produce in the form of raw material, such as metal ores, rubber and unprocessed food. Traditionally, risk-taking activities such as prospecting and mining for natural resources have been organised by MNC's, as has the running of plantations. Increasingly, Third World countries are protesting at the prices they receive for their produce, and also at the role which MNC's have played in exhausting their natural resources. Moves by Third World countries to gain greater control over mining and exploration companies have resulted in a reduction of MNC activity in the Third World.

A recent trend in MNC investment has been to site the most labour-intensive parts of their operations in the Third World. For example, a new laser stereo system may be designed and tested in California, the electrical components made in Scotland, the motor and mechanical parts made in West Germany, and the whole assembled in South Korea for marketing in North America and Europe. Today, 80% of Third World manufactured exports come from just eight countries, two of which are little more than city-states: India, Brazil, Malaysia, Mexico, Hong Kong, Singapore, South Korea and Taiwan. In a study made around 1972, exports of goods manufactured by MNC's accounted for 70% of Singapore's manufactured exports, 43% of Brazil's, and 25-30% of Mexico's.

In these newly industrialising countries, strong and positive government policies have encouraged MNC spread—corporation tax has been waived, hefty royalty fees are paid, free (or almost free) repatriation of company earning is permitted, and in almost every case the government ensures, and will take action to ensure, a compliant workforce.

The Multinational Phenomenon

The final form of MNC production in the Third World is import substitution, whereby an MNC produces locally a product which has previously been imported. This reduces the import bill of the developing country, and provides a captive market for the MNC.

Some benefits obviously do accrue to the local population through wages and increased economic activity, but the experience of Brazil among other countries demonstrates that national income and the gap between rich and poor can increase *together* at a rapid rate. Growth need not necessarily follow that pattern—it can be geared to the needs of the poor. But where MNC's are involved, this distortion seems to be almost inevitable.

Choosing a new pattern

MNC's have come to prominence both in Scotland and in the Third World thanks to modern technology, and the national and international policies of government. Throughout the world, MNC's are now major determinants of policy and practice on employment, income distribution, consumption, including food, types of technology used, and the whole culture within which we live.

Along with the positive factors which have contributed to MNC dominance, there is one factor which has to be listed as having precipitated the rise of MNC's by default, and that is the absence of government intervention in MNC development pattern. The age when iron production was carried out in the back yard, or shoes manufactured by the local artisan, are over; the investment required to win a place in today's market means that only very few institutions are complete. The frequent charge that people simply would not have jobs without IBM or Coats Patons or Caterpillar is true, so long as the government along with the planning agencies, banks, management and workforce, does not offer itself as a catalyst of investment and production.

Although it has been individuals and communities which have suffered from MNC's, they have not been capable of formulating a response. So it remains the duty of political parties and governments to devise policies to control the MNC's in the public interest and to mobilise public support behind them. Policy instruments are not lacking. Domestic production can be encouraged by state buying policy, import controls or trade deals with similarly placed countries to encourage the reconstruction of ailing industries. With respect to investment, the export of finance can be controlled, banks, insurance companies and pension funds can be directed to make at least a proportion of their funds available to industry on a long-term basis, and enterprise funds can be established to assist new business ventures. At the same time new structures of industrial accountability can be explored with the aim of bringing private and institutional shareholders, central and local government and the workforce together in new structures

77

of industrial ownership and control, in Scotland and the Third World. The challenge is formidable. But until it is taken up the multinational producers of biscuits, booze and bandages will hold the stage as the *de facto* planners of our lives.

References

1. D. Hamilton, L. Moar, I. Orton *Job Generation in Scottish Manufacturing Industry*, Fraser of Allander Institute. University of Strathclyde 1981.

2. Quoted in Lewis D. Solomon *Multinational companies and the emerging world order*, Kennikat Press 1978 on the basis of figures in *Multinational Corporations in World Development*, Department of Economic and Social Affairs, United Nations.

3. Quoted in R. Barnett and R. Muller *Global Reach: the power of the multinational corporations* on the basis of figures in *The Multinational Corporation and the World Economy*, United States Senate Finance Committee 1973.

4. *US Direct Investment Abroad*, US Department of Commerce 1981.

5. *US Direct Investment Position Abroad—Income by Country 1970-79*, Statistical Abstract of the United States 1980, Department of Commerce Bureau of Statistics.

6. *The United Kingdom as a Tax Haven*, Special Report No. 95 Economist Intelligence Unit. 1981.

7. L.W. Rogers *Marketing in a Competitive Economy*, New York: International Publications 1969.

8. *The Ownership of Scottish Manufacturing Industry*, Scottish Council Research Institute, Edinburgh May 1980.

9. Deepak Nayyer *Transnational Corporations and Manufactured Exports from Poor Countries*, Economic Journal 1978.

TABLE 1—Ten Leading Scottish Multinational Companies

Company	Position in The Times top 1000	Main products	No. of employees	International activities
Burmah Oil	41	Oil	17,000 U.K. 15,000 rest of the world	Subsidiary companies in Liberia. Bermuda, Seychelles, Australia, Brazil, U.S.A., S. Africa, Sweden—to name a few.
Distillers	59	Whisky	19,000 U.K.	60% of turnover is ex-U.K.
United Biscuits	69	Biscuits, cakes	41,000 U.K.	Exports worth £21m. per year. Subsidiaries in U.S.A. and Europe. associated company in Japan.
Coats Patons	85	Threads, yarns, clothing	23,000 U.K. 42,000 rest of the world	25% of total assets employed in S. America, Africa, Asia and Australia. This 25% provides 44% of profit.
Stenhouse Holdings	151	Insurance brokers	5,100	Has 161 offices in 32 countries, including U.S.A., Canada, Papua New Guinea, Fiji, Singapore, S. Africa, Malaysia.
Arthur Bell & Sons	244	Whisky	1,932 U.K.	Has 6% of world whisky market. All companies operate in U.K. except Bell & Sons (Bermuda) Ltd.
Low & Bonar	284	Packing. engineering. textiles	9,300	Principle activities: packaging in U.K. and Canada. engineering in U.K., Kenya and S. Africa. textiles in U.K., Belgium, Kenya, Nigeria S. Africa and Zambia.
Weir Group Ltd	287	Engineers	8,539 U.K.	32% of profit contributed by overseas subsidiaries. Exports worth £65m. from U.K. each year.Major markets in N. America and Middle East.
Wm. Baird	324	Textiles, industrial investment	12,837	Wholly-owned subsidiaries in Hong Kong, Australia, S. Africa and W. Germany
Jas. Finlay	433	International traders & financiers	1,938 U.K.	Operations in Africa & Asia rep. 45% of group turnover and 82% of pre-tax profits.

The Multinational Phenomenon

TABLE 2—Scottish Council Research Institute

Scottish Manufacturing Employment, by ownership and industrial sector, 1973.

	Scottish(%)	Other U.K.(%)	European(%)	North America(%)	Other & Joint(%)	Total
Food, Drink & Tobacco	48.3	44.5	1.5	5.7		100.0
Coal & petroleum products	15.4	80.2	—	—	4.4	100.0
Chemicals & allied industries	11.8	63.2	10.7	12.1	2.2	100.0
Metal Manufacture	18.3	70.4	—	2.2	9.1	100.0
Mechanical Engineering	39.0	29.1	1.8	29.3	0.7	100.0
Instrument Engineering	16.9	21.1	—	60.7	1.3	100.0
Electrical Engineering	7.8	52.4	8.3	31.4	0.1	100.0
Shipbuilding & Marine eng	53.3	29.8	—	11.8	5.1	100.0
Vehicles	9.8	53.3	0.5	36.4	—	100.0
Other Metal Goods	58.6	25.2	0.5	10.9	1.9	100.0
Textiles	64.2	28.8	3.6	3.0	0.4	100.0
Leather Goods	88.0	12.0	—	—	—	100.0
Clothing & Footwear	48.2	38.0	—	13.8	—	100.0
Bricks, Pottery etc.	37.1	48.1	—	1.2	13.6	100.0
Timber, Furniture etc.	87.2	12.4	—	0.4	—	100.0
Paper & Printing	55.0	39.4	0.8	2.5	2.3	100.0
Other Manufacturing	28.4	43.2	1.5	26.1	0.8	100.0
Totals:	41.2	39.8	2.1	14.9	2.0	100.0
Adjusted for non-response	43.9	38.6	2.0	13.7	1.8	100.0

TABLE 3—Scottish Manufacturing Employment by Ownership and Industrial sector, 1979.

	Scottish	Other U.K.(%)	European(%)	North America(%)	Other & Joint(%)	Total
Food, Drink & Tobacco	46.4	42.1	1.9	9.6	—	100.0
Coal & Petroleum products	11.7	88.3	—	—	—	100.0
Chemicals & Allied industries	8.3	70.9	8.7	12.1	—	100.0
Metal Manufacture	16.6	77.4	—	5.9	0.1	100.0
Mechanical Engineering	58.1	16.9	1.5	21.3	2.1	100.0
Instrument Engineering	3.1	19.0	0.0	77.9	—	100.0
Electrical Engineering	12.4	42.9	9.8	34.7	0.2	100.0
Shipbuilding & Marine Engineering	14.6	81.8	0.1	3.5	—	100.0
Vehicles & Aerospace	6.2	65.0	25.0	3.9	—	100.0
Other metal goods	55.6	31.7	2.7	6.1	3.9	100.0
Textiles	76.2	22.0	0.9	0.9	—	100.0
Leather Goods	75.5	21.5	3.0	—	—	100.0
Clothing & Footwear	45.8	38.4	0.1	15.1	0.6	100.0
Bricks, Pottery etc.	18.8	34.0	0.2	1.6	45.4	100.0
Timber, Furniture etc.	79.8	17.1	2.3	0.9	—	100.0
Paper & Printing	52.6	42.6	1.7	3.1	—	100.0
Other Manufacturing	27.6	38.4	12.3	20.3	1.5	100.0
Totals:	38.8	39.6	3.9	14.7	2.9	100.0
Adjusted for non-response	40.4	38.9	3.8	14.0	2.8	100.0

(Proportions may not sum to 100.0 because of rounding)

MULTINATIONALS, SCOTLAND, AND THE THIRD WORLD: THE CHANGING REALITY

by John R. Firn

Introduction

There are few institutions in the contemporary world as controversial as the modern multinational corporation (MNC). The impact and role of such enterprises in the growth and modernisation of developing nations generates much debate and research but no generally accepted conclusions. The balance of belief at present is that MNC's, if left to their own unregulated actions and devices, exhibit tendencies to exploit their host nations, especially in the countries of the South, and that because of this there is a need to introduce an international regulatory regime to combat the monopolistic, restrictive and exploitative practices of the MNC's. Such an international investment regime is proposed in The Brandt Report,[1] and has now become an essential component in the policy statements of most international organisations concerned with economic and social development in Third World nations.

The continued development of MNC's and of multinational business that will occur in the remaining years of this century does seem to point to the need for some form of international supervision, but the complexities of multinational economic activities together with the current international poltical disarray offer few prospects of an effective and accepted regulatory regime for international investment in the immediate future. Thus both Third World nations and Scotland are faced with the dilemma of formulating policy approaches for economic development that of necessity require the active involvement and participation of MNC's whilst being powerless fully to control the impact and direction of their activities, even supposing that a sufficient knowledge of the economics of MNC's existed. However, it is this writer's view that the case against MNC's as overt or covert exploiters of the nations of the South has not been conclusively demonstrated, and that the traditional Scottish verdict of "not proven" is perhaps appropriate.

The purpose of this essay is not to review in depth the impact of MNC's on Scotland and the Third World, but rather to provide a perspective on the links between the MNC's, Scotland and the nations of the South. This challenging topic has so far escaped the attention of academic or other investigators, despite its importance for the future of Scotland. Normally economists regard this type of subject area with relish, but in practice the modern MNC poses a real difficulty for research and it has proved exceedingly difficult to apply modern, or indeed traditional, theories and models to it, and thus to construct realistic policy measures to guide its development.

The principal problem is that the MNC is both an element in its domestic national economy and a factor in the broader international economy: this breaches the basic assumption of existing economic theory that the firm is a subordinate and dependent component of the larger national economy. If we ignore this little problem for the present, and simply look at MNC's, we can see that the reality is no less complex.

The Concept of MNC's

In any discussion of MNC's it is important at the outset to realise that they are a far from homogeneous group. It is therefore impossible to consider MNC's as merely being a collection of large, US-owned enterprises of the Coca-Cola, Ford, IBM or Exxon type. In practice, MNC's demonstrate a truly bewildering variety of organisational, ownership, operational and functional types, each of which presents different challenges and opportunities to host nations.

Five main types of MNC's have developed during the past four hundred years. In broad chronological order these are:

(i)   Colonial Companies: These are enterprises that have their origin in the colonial system, perhaps typified by the British East India Company. Such MNC's, which are now virtually extinct (save perhaps in the Eastern Bloc), had a primary function of extracting raw materials for the metropolitan country and simultaneously monopolising the colony's market for finished goods. Many Scottish-based MNC's established in the late 19th century came within this category.

(ii)   Resource-based Companies: Such MNC's, which are a continuing source of political conflict, especially in South America and Africa, are orientated towards extracting raw materials and natural resources. The multinational oil companies, in which Scotland has more than a passing interest, are a special sub-category and are the most visible of this group, but mining, timber and agricultural enterprises also are important participants in the economies of many South nations. The potential conflict here is between the host nation's desire to control the exploitation of natural resources, and the continuing demand for raw materials by consuming nations.

(iii)   Public Untility Companies: this is a small, specialised but complex set of MNC's, typified by the existence of a high degree of monopoly in the markets where they operate. Electric power, telephone and transport companies are the usual form, and Scottish capital has been active in establishing many of these enterprises in developing nations, most of which are now state-owned.

(iv) Manufacturing Concerns: Since the end of the Second World War manufacturing MNC's have come to typify MNC's as a whole, although in some cases, Singer's, late of Clydebank, for example, their existence dates back over a century. It is to such companies that developing nations in the South, and depressed regions in the industrial world, have looked for economic growth. Governments have designed complex and comprehensive incentive programmes to attract their investments. Major beneficiaries of these incentive programmes have been the holders of the equity in the parent companies who have seen much of their company's development cost provided or underwritten by tax-payers in other countries—a frequently neglected consideration.

(v) Service and Tertiary Sector Companies: The continuing shift away from manufacturing in North nations means that service and tertiary sector companies may well become the dominant type of MNC in the future. The essential factors to host economies will be finance, management, and technological expertise. Thus joint ventures will be more important with this type of company, which will ease their acceptance by host governments.

The situation is further complicated, however, by the fact that in each of the above broad categories (and there are some MNC conglomerate companies that are active in all, such as Lonrho), a wide range of organisational types of MNC exist. Some companies are tightly centralised and controlled from the headquarters country; others are highly decentralised and operate as domestic firms in the host economy; while yet others are sufficiently large and powerful to transcend national borders and thus form a complex system which is really only answerable to itself. Each of these organisational types has its own potential and problems.

The study of MNC's is further complicated by the fact they they can no longer be regarded as essentially a United States, and more recently a European, phenomenon. There is now a growing number of MNC's operating from Third World nations, especially those of the small group of Newly Industrialised Countries (NIC's) such as Brazil, Mexico and South Korea. Another set of MNC's is emerging from the Soviet Bloc countries, some of which have already become major presences in certain industrial sectors, and outside the communist nations, an increasing role is being played by state-owned, public-sector MNC's, which may have objectives and operating patterns very different from private sector MNC's. Finally, it is no longer possible to assume that all MNC's are large, complex industrial companies, for the combination of declining costs of communications and increasing tariff barriers has recently encouraged the emergence of a new breed of relatively small MNC's which in the long-term may challenge the large established international corporations.

Multinationals, Scotland and the Third World

When examining the future impact of MNC's upon Scotland and the Third World, this diversity must be borne in mind if analysis and policy are to be relevant. The complex patterns of MNC's might suggest that policy analysis is impossible, but if the focus is switched to individual industrial sectors, and more specifically, to particular commodity and product markets, it is possible to establish the roles and contributions of MNC's in such a way as to consider policy responses and initiatives.

The Concept of the South

Before considering the relationship of Scotland and the Third World to MNC's it is necessary briefly to state that the South as an economic and political concept is almost as meaningless as that of MNC. The range of economic and political systems, performances, problems and potential are every bit as varied as the types of MNC, and it makes little sense to regard Singapore or Korea as being truly comparable to Bangladesh or Ethiopia, or any of these to Kuwait. This is especially important in the context of considering the so-called challenge to nations such as Scotland from the producers of the South. Again, a sensible approach is required which focusses analysis and policy at specific market sectors rather than broad national groupings.

Scotland, MNC's and the Third World

Scotland's own experience offers a unique perspective of MNC's, which if properly considered could yield potentially important lessons both for the nations of the South, and for her own economic future. This uniqueness stems from the switch that has taken place during the past three-quarters of a century from Scotland being a nation that contained the headquarters of a relatively large number of economically and technologically influential MNC's that played important roles in the development of many overseas countries, to one whose current and foreseeable economic development is largely dependent upon the fortunes of MNC's that are controlled in other parts of the world, principally in the rest of the UK and the United States. The switch has, of course, not been total, for there are still a number of Scottish-based MNC's at the forefront of their sectors in the international economy, but the balance has clearly changed.

The prime focus of this essay is not on the long-term implications of this changing balance, but on the triangular relationship between Scotland, the MNC's and the Third World. There are three main issues involved which are each worth brief discussion: the stability of the MNC's that presently exist in Scotland, and especially the fear that their operations will be internally switched to locations in the South; the competition between Scotland and Third World nations for MNC investment and plants; and the potential competition to Scottish-based companies from multinational production located in Third World nations.

Multinationals, Scotland and the Third World

(i) The Stability of MNC's in Scotland

Whilst the experience of Scotland in the post-war period has shown that MNC's in Scotland do sometimes close down their operations because of intra-company changes in production structures or because of changes in demand, there is very little evidence that any of the closures that have taken place have been through the direct transfer of operations to cheaper locations in Third World nations. A more usual pattern has been that MNC's in sectors such as electronics have developed Scottish and Third World locations in parallel, with Scottish produced parts and components being assembled in the cheaper labour cost plants of the South. The classic example of this are the integrated circuit wafers produced by electronics MNC's in Scotland which are subsequently assembled and packaged by workers in their Asian plants.

A more widespread difficulty has been that the older established MNC's have sometimes neglected to install new plant and machinery in Scottish plants. But in such cases the new investment that has taken place has been into other European locations closer to where the market is, rather than in Third World nations. The importance of the European market in the decision to locate in Scotland effectively ensures that locations here are not directly challenged by the South.

A full understanding of the production and marketing relationships of Scottish-based MNC's would require a sectoral approach to be adopted, which is obviously outside the scope of this essay. But one sector that is often discussed in the context of potential switching of operations between the North and the South is electronics, and it is worth briefly examining potential developments here.

Whilst most of the assembly of electronics products is currently undertaken in Third World nations, the future development of the industry is toward more technological content and increasing capital intensity, with the big constraints being the shortage of electrical and electronic engineers, and more importantly of highly skilled producers of the increasingly important softwear that enables electronics hardware to operate. These factors, together with the tariff barriers to imports and special national electronics programmes which are becoming universal in all industrial nations, together point to a continued concentration of the electronics industry, especially the production of more advanced components, in the existing electronics locations such as Scotland. The rapid development of Singapore and Korea in electronics assembly has also led to skill shortages there and a gradual erosion of their cheap labour status, although the NIC's will remain formidable competitors in certain sub-sectors of consumer electronics.

(ii) Scottish and South Competition for MNC's

The fear has been expressed that Scotland is moving into an era of competition with Third World countries for new MNC investment. However, in general the types of MNC's that consider location in these two areas are completely different. There are some exceptions, where a parent MNC may consider Singapore, Puerto Rico, Eire and Scotland for its new plant, but these are few and far between. The usual competition to Scotland for mobile investment comes from other European nations, and more especially from other areas in the European periphery. Indeed rather than competition there has been the development within certain manufacturing MNC's of an integrated partnership between US, European and Third World locations.

(iii)   The Competition from Third World MNC's

Fears have also been expressed that Scottish companies will face increasing competition from Third World producers in many sectors such as textiles and consumer goods, and that among these Third World producers are the major Western MNC's. This is a topic that is more properly dealt with in the context of trade liberalisation, but the evidence so far is that the most effective competition has come from smaller and medium-sized domestic companies in Third World locations, although hidden subsidiaries of Japanese multinational groups and public-sector companies in a number of developing nations are also growing factors in world markets. It does appear likely that large and powerful indigenous MNC's based in Korea, Hong Kong and Singapore will become much more effective competitors in the near future, as well as the foreign-exchange dominated MNC's from the Soviet bloc whose competition is much more difficult to counter, especially when their modern production equipment has been purchased from Western nations, often through barter deals.

The correct response to such competition (if the problems of dumping are excluded) is to concentrate on maximising the competitive advantages in areas where leadership is retained or can be developed, although it must be accepted that the positive adjustment measures that such an approach assumed are not likely to be adopted during a global economic recession.

The Future Perspective

Paradoxically, the slower rate of economic growth now anticipated, and the consequent increase in neo-mercantilist protectionist measures, is likely to generate an increase in the number of MNC's, as international companies realise that access to such protected markets will only be possible through production inside previous export markets. This is likely to ensure a continued flow of new MNC operations to host countries such as Scotland and the Third World, especially of the newer high technology companies established in the late 1960's that have now begun to enter overseas markets. This continued flow, which however will not be at the high levels seen in the 1950s and 1960s when multinational business acted as a major source of growth in the world economy, will present both opportunities and problems for Scotland and the Third World, and as such more effort must be made in understanding the needs and motivations of MNC's, and their impact on host nations. For example it is clearly important to distinguish between new inward investments by MNC's in a host nation, and the take-over of growing indigenous companies by MNC's: even the United States, the traditional home of acquisitive MNC's, erects barriers to take-overs of domestic companies.

It is important, given the likely future investment and trade environment, to consider whether a conscious effort should be mounted to assist the development of further Scottish owned MNC's as a means of penetrating the markets that are being closed off by tariff barriers. So far the understanding of the opportunities for Scottish companies in terms of joint-ventures with Third World companies appears to have been limited, although a small number of Scottish enterprises, expecially in textiles, have even progressed to outward processing of their products in countries such as Hong Kong.

Scotland, if it can persuade its remaining domestic companies to adopt an aggressive, outward-looking trading and investment perspective that recognises the gains to be had from partnership between itself and nations of the Third World, can face the long-term future with some optimism, despite the immediate bleak economic outlook. It is conceivable that the major areas of potential for Scottish companies lie within the hugh domestic markets of the Third World, although the development of such markets is heavily dependent upon a more enlightened and progressive UK aid policy: in this context it is worth bearing in mind that much of Scotland's nineteenth century economic development was fuelled by the provision of Scottish capital to enterprises in colonial countries which was then used to purchase Scottish products.

Against this there is the need to develop sensible policies towards the continued growth of MNC's within Scotland, in order to ensure that their long-term net contribution to the Scottish economy remains as positive as it has been in the past. The economic history of Scotland demonstrates clearly that many of the nation's structural and performance problems are due to internal causes and factors, and thus cannot be blamed on the activities of MNC's, Third World countries, or any combination of the two. A close reading of the Brandt Report does reveal that beyond all the undoubted problems there are real opportunities for Scotland to participate profitably in the developing of the Third World in a non-exploitive sense. A better understanding of our own past development is a fundamental requirement for such participation.

THE POLITICAL ECONOMY OF THE
THE THIRD WORLD INDUSTRIALISATION:
THE IMPLICATIONS FOR SCOTLAND.

by John R. Firn

NOTE: The analysis, interpretation and opinions expressed in this paper are personal ones, and thus should not be attributed to the Scottish Development Agency nor seen as a statement of the Agency's policies or views. The contents of the paper should also not be quoted without the author's permission.

Introduction

One of the most visible and persistent features of economic development during the past two decades has been the growing integration of national and international economic and political systems. This phenomenon is now widely recognised as a major influence on the domestic and external policies of most individual nation states, no matter what their size or level of development. The causes, dimension and implications of such integration are gradually becoming better understood, especially as the analytical power of international relations (now a recognisably distinct and respected discipline within the social sciences) has become both more comprehensive and more sophisticated, especially with regard to the empirical measurement of such relationships.

A fundamental consequence of such increasing integration, and one that has especial relevance when examining the relationships between Scotland, the Third World and multinational enterprises, is that it implies a substantial reduction in the real power of states to act independently of one another, and thus there has been a marked erosion in the ability of countries to fully command both the pace and direction of their own economic, political and social development. There have been many signs recently that individuals and nations have become alarmed at the long-term implications of continued integration, and this concern has been increasingly transformed into direct national policy initiatives by a number of countries (Britain included) anxious to re-assert a greater degree of control and sovereignty over their own affairs, especially in relation to economic development. It should be noted here that this is also an important feature of the prevailing economic policy philosophies that are being discussed in relation to the Scottish economy, although for reasons which will become clear in this paper, it is an option which is exceedingly difficult to implement.

As might be expected in a period characterised by a relatively severe international economic recession, many of the influential analyses that have been undertaken of the effects of economic and political integration have concentrated on the negative aspects and impacts as they affect individual countries or multinational groupings. Far less attention has been devoted to the identification and development of the positive beneficial effects that can still ensue from closer international cooperation. It is not the intention of this paper to examine this apparent asymmetricality in analysis and policy evaluation, but rather to examine a comparatively neglected aspect of international relations, namely the relationship that exists between a region within a nation state and the countries of the Third World. It has to be admitted at once that the analysis of such an esoteric set of relationships is not one that might suggest itself to social scientists or policy makers, but in the case of Scotland, it might well offer us some new insights into the nature of the local economic and political systems, and also provide us with a greater degree of understanding of the possibilities that may exist for Scotland and the Scots to play a more effective role in the development of the Third World.

This paper will therefore concentrate on the development of industrialisation in Third World nations, and the impact that this will have on Scotland. It will also look at the opportunities that are open to Scottish industry to become involved in this industrialisation process.

Third World Nations and the International Economy

It is impossible in an essay such as this to examine the complete development experience of the Third World in the post-war period. What follows is therefore a selective overview of the main features of the economic growth of the developing countries, especially as they relate to the main theme of industrialisation. It is also necessary to stress here that it is dangerous in the extreme to assume that the nations comprising the Third World are a homogeneous grouping, for in practice every country is unique in its structure, performance, potential and problems. However, there is broad agreement that the Third World can now be divided up into two main groups of nations, the Low Income Countries (LIC) comprising 38 nations whose GNP per capita in 1978 ranged from $90 (Bangladesh) to the $300 and the 51 Middle Income Countries (MIC) where the average 1978 per capita income was $1,250, ranging from Egypt's $390 to Israel's $3,500.[1] There is also broad agreement that at least 15 of the MIC nations are well on the way to joining the ranks of the industrialised nations, and as such these can be seen as forming a separate group of semi-industrialised nations.

The growth record of the Third World countries since 1950 has been relatively impressive, with income per capita growing by just under 3% p.a. over the 1950-1975 period, with an acceleration to 3.4% p.a. in the 1960's. Although comparable statistical records for the period before 1950 are sparse and unreliable, there seems little doubt that this recent growth performance is far in excess of their long-term historical development, and further it compares very favourably indeed with the economic growth-rates that were attained by the present developed nations during their main industrialisation phase between 1850 and 1950. Yet the overall performance of the Third World nations hides a wide range of disparities in growth rates: a number of countries, such as Bhutan, Somalia, Bangladesh, Niger, and Senegal have had **negative** rates of growth over the past 18 years. Further the LIC nations, (with a 0.9% p.a. growth in GNP per capita between 1960-1976), have been slowly falling behind the MIC nations (who have achieved a 2.8% p.a. GNP per capita growth over the same period), and both groups of countries have fallen behind the 3.4% growth rate in per capita incomes achieved by the industrial nations. A prime cause of these widening gaps has been the continuation of rapid population growth assisted by the increased access to improved medical facilities. As a result, the economic growth that has been achieved has been neither rapid enough nor comprehensive enough to reduce substantially the number of people in the Third World who live in absolute poverty. This simple fact is something that must be continually borne in mind when we discuss the response of nations such as Scotland to the challenge of Third World industrialisation, for it will be the poorer inhabitants of these nations who will bear the brunt of any sharply restrictive measures that might be introduced.

Within the overall economic growth that has been achieved by the Third World countries, there has been a marked shift in their economic structure away from a dependence on agriculture towards the industrial and service sectors. In both LIC and MIC nations between 1960 and 1975, the industrial sectors grew at consistently faster rates than GDP: in LIC countries industry expanded at an average annual rate of 5.4% against a GDP growth of 3.1%, whilst in MIC's industry expanded at 7.9% compared to GDP rates that averaged 6.0%. During the same period, the industrial sectors of the developed nations such as Britain rose by 4.7%, and thus they were able to maintain overall dominance in world industrial production, even though in many developed countries the relative share of the industrial sectors in the overall economy declined. This expansion of the industrial sectors of Third World nations has continued into the 1970's, but in common with the industrial growth in the developed nations it has slowed substantially following the post-1973 international recession.

The fast growth-rates achieved by the industrial sectors of the developing nations between 1960 and 1976, resulted in the share of such sectors in the overall GDP of the economies involved rising from 12 to 19% in LIC nations, and from 23 to 32% in MIC countries, whilst in the industrial nations the share of industry has remained constant and even declined in countries such as the UK. Once again, it should be remembered that the grouped figures conceal very wide disparities in the performance of individual countries, and in the growth rates achieved by the individual industrial sectors within each country. Further, it must be borne in mind that the low industrial growth-rates achieved by some Third World countries, such as India's 3.8% between 1960 and 1975, represent large amounts of industrial goods, whereas the high growth rates found in other developing nations have been achieved with only relatively small increases in the volume and value measures of industrial production. The figures also understate the real increase in industrial power made available to Third World nations as they make no real allowance for the sharp increase in the quality and technological effectiveness of many Third World industrial products.

The main factor behind the expansion of the industrial potential of Third World nations has been their growing ability to obtain funds necessary to finance the purchase of capital equipment. Both LIC and MIC nations have managed to raise their rates of Gross Domestic Investment since 1960. The poorer LIC countries' success in pushing their rate of investment up to 15% of GDP is particularly noteworthy because it was achieved despite serious taxation problems, difficulties in finding profitable investment opportunities, and deficiencies of management and administrative skills. MIC nations have done even better. By 1976, they had pushed their investment rate up to 24% of GDP, about the same level as that achieved in the industrial nations although still below the 33% reached by Japan in 1976, and the 35% produced by the development of oil and gas reserves in Norway.

In both LIC and MIC countries, this rise in capital investment has been helped by inflows of both private capital and official development assistance (overseas aid). External funds have been equivalent to about 17% of gross domestic investment in Third World countries. This external capital, whilst playing a major role in the industrialisation efforts of many nations, has, however, not been without its own problems, principally that the terms on which it has been made available have led to many nations building up large external debts to the industrial nations and international institutions. By the end of 1980, it was estimated that the total outstanding debt of 96 developing nations (including undisbursed funds) came to $260 bn, and consequently the burden of servicing such debts (i.e. paying the interest and amortization charges) meant that a large proportion of the export earnings of Third World countries were diverted away from further investment and personal consumption.

Industrialisation in the Third World

The reasons behind the ambition of developing nations to expand their industrial sectors and raise the level and quality of their industrial output are complex. For most countries there is at least an element of political self-respect involved—real nations have modern industries. But for many developing nations there is a strong economic rationale for building up a manufacturing sector based on cheap raw materials, a plentiful supply of labour; and a growing managerial capability. In fact, there is some

91

justification for arguing that many manufactured goods would be most efficiently produced in developing nations to be sold to the developed nations in return for the produce of their efficient agricultural industries. However, a major force in the drive to industrialisation has been the need of many Third World countries to reduce the outflows of scarce foreign exhange caused by imports of capital goods and consumer goods, and the need to provide employment opportunities for a growing labour force.

In the 1950's those few Third World nations that took the industrialisation route seriously, usually attempted to compete with the industrialised nations by adopting their technology and size of production units. For many countries the consequences of this were severe. Even where sufficient internal capital and foreign aid was available to allow a nation to build large-scale steel or petrochemical complexes, lack of managerial experience, shortages of power, inefficient transport, the cost of maintaining the plants and purchasing spares, the need to service the loans and repay capital, and the failure to improve the supply of local inputs and raw materials (especially in the agricultural sectors), meant that many of the large complexes that were developed were a net drain on the national economy rather than a real contributor to economic development. The experience of India during the second Five Year Plan is a prime example of this, and students of development economics would do well to study the lessons of this: indeed such experiences have a message for those interested in the future growth of the Scottish economy.

It is perhaps fair to point out that, with some notable exceptions— principally in those nations where internal politics and military adventures have been encouraged—these lessons have been heeded, and the current range of industrial development programmes that are being implemented are more realistic and better related to resources. Large-scale industrial complexes have become more reliable and technologically easier to manage, but more importantly increased attention has been given to agricultural production and to the encouragement of small-scale production methods employing simple or appropriate technology suitable for rural areas. The renewed emphasis on small-scale industrialisation, which has its counterpart in the recent switch of policy towards the small firm sector in industrial nations such as the United Kingdom, has been based on the argument that small units are not only more labour-intensive, but also produce more goods per unit of land and per unit of fixed investment. Again, the case of India is an interesting example of this, where between 1978 and 1980 the Janata Party government attempted to give priority to Gandhian rural cottage industry, whilst investing heavily in agriculture.

There is one other important point to note about the nature of industrialisation in Third World countries. Many of the main domestic producing companies are state-owned, or state controlled or regulated. This is almost universally so in large-scale high technology industries such as petroleum refining, steel production and heavy engineering. It follows that there is a strong political element that has to be taken into account in any analysis of industrial production or trade. Indeed, the share of world trade that is accounted for by bilateral deals between public-sector corporations is rising sharply in both the industrial nations and the developing world, and with it the likelihood of trade agreements based on political rather than economic considerations.

Once industrialisation has reached a certain level in a developing nation, the pressure to export the goods that are produced grows. The driving force behind an increase in exports may be the need to obtain foreign exchange; the limited capacity of the domestic economy to absorb the goods that are produced; or simply the market attractions of other countries, especially the industrial nations. In some cases, the producing governments assist exporters by allowing them tax concessions on exports, by giving them a direct subsidy for exported goods or by helping the producing companies with export finance and guarantees. When these incentives are combined with low production costs the Third World product can be highly competitive in world markets—as long as the importing countries are prepared to allow free entry. However, as we shall see, this has increasingly not been the case.

The Growth of Third World Manufactured Exports

One of the most important features of the post-war international economy has been the continuous expansion of international trade. Since 1960, the imports of industrial nations have risen by over 7% per annum. This expansion has been mainly the result of three factors: institutional developments, technological innovations, and demographic trends.

The changing institutional framework has been perhaps the most important cause of increasing international trade, and at the centre of this has been the progressive movement towards a more liberal world trading system enshrined in the GATT reached just after the end of the second world war, which marked a determined attempt to avoid the chaotic trading environment that had characterised the 1920's and 1930's. GATT introduced a foreign trade system based on reciprocity and non-discrimination, provided a set of regulations within which trade should be conducted, and also a mechanism for further attempts at trade liberalisation. Further liberalisation was achieved via the various Kennedy and other rounds of negotiations, and by the early 1970's the weighted average tariff for the major trading nations had been reduced to a mere 7.7% on all industrial products. These reductions, assisted by the relatively stable international monetary framework that existed until the oil crisis, resulted in the international trade growing by 600% between 1948 and 1973.

The Political Economy

Cost-reducing technology, which became widely available to Third World nations during the late 1950's, was another important factor lying behind the growth in world trade. The expansion of the labour force in developing countries in the post-war period, which brought about a marked shift in the comparative advantage of Third World nations in those manufacturing industries requiring large amounts of low-skilled labour, and the more efficient use of skilled labour in developed countries, was the other main factor that encouraged world trade.

The developing nations of the Third World have taken full advantage of this liberal trade environment, and between 1960 and 1975, the manufactured exports of these countries rose by an average of 12.3% per annum (against 8.8% for the industrial nations). Whereas in 1960, manufactured goods accounted for only about 13% of the total non-petroleum exports of Third World nations, by 1976 this figure had risen to nearly 43%. The growing share of the developing nations in total world trade in manufactured exports has enabled many Third World countries to reduce their previous precarious dependence on primary products. The last two decades have seen developing nations begin to protect their trading futures further by diversifying out of basic manufactures such as textiles to made up clothing, steel, electronics and chemicals.

There are a number of interesting points to note about the manufactured exports from the Third World. First, these exports are dominated by a relatively small number of the semi-industrialised nations such as Korea, Taiwan, Spain and Hong Kong, who account for about 45% of Third World exports, while the addition of another 8 countries (Brazil, Greece, India, Israel, Mexico, Portugal, Singapore and Yugoslavia) raises the export concentration ratio to over 80%. Second, by 1978, there were over 50 nations of the Third World exporting manufactured goods worth $500m per annum, and 17 countries had manufactured export worth over $5,000m. Third, these exports were concentrated in a relatively small number of commodity classes, of which textiles were absolutely the most important.

The above dimensions of the growth of manufactured exports by Third World countries are impressive, and they are seen as a severe threat to the industrial capacity of the developed nations, especially in the member nations of the EEC, who, as we shall see, have been among the leaders of those demanding protection. Yet, there is a real danger that a relatively few instances of industrial damage resulting from Third World imports of this type will blind us to the fact that the share of developing countries in the total domestic consumption of manufactured goods in industrial countries is still very small indeed: it had risen from a miniscule 0.4% in 1960 to only 1.2% by 1975, (under 3% in the United Kingdom in 1980). If it is assumed that trade barriers remain roughly as they are at present (a dangerous assumption in the present political maelstrom), then the World Bank estimates that by

The Political Economy

1985, this share will only have risen to about 2.7%, which certainly does not seem to present a major challenge to the industrial future of industrial nations.

It should also be borne in mind that much of the gains that the Third World have made from increasing manufactured exports have been wiped out or "devalued" by the erosion in their terms of trade caused by the falling real prices received for their agricultural and other commodity exports in the 1960's and 1970's.

These declines have been caused by the low income elasticity of demand for such primary products (chiefly beverages such as tea and coffee, and hard fibres) in the developed countries, and an inattention to their efficient production. But, despite the restricted nature of the present challenge from Third World producers of manufactured goods, companies in the industrial nations have felt under increasing threat. Consequently there has been a sharp increase in protectionist measures in the developed nations since 1973, and these are worth a brief examination.

The Growth of Protectionism

The favourable attitudes in the industrial nations towards tariff reductions that were a major factor in the large growth in international trade in the post 1950 period, were effectively ended by the severe and persistent global economic recession that began in 1974-75. This sudden check to world growth, which was only partly due to the fourfold increase in world oil prices in 1973-74, brought in its train a whole range of protectionist actions and schemes.

The main participants in this move towards protectionism, which can be defined as the desire to protect a country's home industries from the effects of foreign competition, were the members of the EEC, Canada, the United States and Japan, who between them account for approximately 60% of world trade. However, other smaller industrial nations and many developing countries also introduced restrictions on international trade, and the continued inability of the world economy to pull out of the post-1973 slowdown has meant that protectionist measures have become both persistent and widespread.

The types of protectionist measures currently employed include the invocation of "escape clauses" by individual nations to impose tariffs and/or quotas on imports that are seen as threatening their domestic industries; the use of anti-dumping or counter-vailing measures (such as the USA's introduction of a minimum 'trigger price' below which steel imports are restricted); the use of non-tariff measures (i.e. health; technical; safety standards; measurements); and the negotiation of bilateral trade agreements with those countries whose exports are seen as posing a threat: these latter frequently

95

outside the existing rules of organisations such as GATT and thus hard to control.

So far, the trade measures taken by the industrialised nations have been restricted to a comparatively few sectors (clothing and textiles; electrical consumer goods; footwear; steel; shipbuilding; and certain metal products such as cutlery), and their main impact has been concentrated on a relatively small number of developing nations (Korea being a principal target) and Japan. But although the measures taken are not yet widespread, their appearance is ominous for developing nations in the Third World because the sectors involved are those where such countries already have or are developing a degree of comparative advantage, and thus any expansion in the coverage or the severity of the restrictions would seriously affect the long-term export prospects of Third World nations. If this happens it will also have an impact on the import programmes of developing nations, and as they currently account for about 26% of the export markets of the industrial nations, the overall effect on world trade could be disastrous.

The ability of industrial nations to resist internal political pressures for the imposition of protective measures is often fairly low, especially where any threat from imports is concentrated on a relatively small sector, or where it affects a particular region whose economic future depends on the maintenance of a particular industrial activity. It can also be weakened if the sector is one where there is temporary excess capacity, especially if much of the installed equipment is relatively modern and potentially very productive. This latter problem is one that has become of crucial importance in relation to both European shipbuilding and steel production.

Political economists in the major international institutions have worked hard at trying to persuade individual nations of the benefits of trade liberalisation, and have written sophisticated analyses outlining the benefits in terms of resulting economies of scale; the improved competitive position of domestic industries; and greater domestic and international price stability. However, these sophisticated and worthy appraisals of the potential benefits of increased free trade do not carry much weight in the context of an international economic recession, where high levels of unemployment and low levels of capacity utilisation exist.

There is nevertheless a slow realisation that moves will eventually have to be made to remove protectionist measures, and that if this is to be done, there will be a need to develop internal economic and industrial policies in the developed nations that will begin to adjust the existing industrial structures away from sectors and products that can be most economically produced in Third World nations, towards industries where the advantages lie with the industrial nations. Such policies may well be difficult to introduce, especially as there is an asymmetry in the pressures for protection: the industries that are under threat are often well organised, informed and effective pressure groups, whereas the consuming public at large—who would benefit most by trade liberalisation—are usually uninformed, widely dispersed, and hard to organise.

Implications for Scotland

The post-war growth in international industrialisation has important consequences for Scotland, especially as we have an economy with a number of sectors such as textiles, steel and shipbuilding that are potentially very exposed to the export challenge of the Third World nations. The critical point for informed discussion within Scotland today should be how we should respond to such a challenge. It is a personal belief that any policy response that we consider should be based on a positive attitude towards change: in other words, we should avoid and reject any moves to impose a greater degree of isolation and protection in order to support the older declining industries.

There are a number of reasons for this. First, there are a large number of industrial and commercial enterprises in Scotland that require absolutely no protection at all, except perhaps from purely disruptive short-term competitive effects, most of which stem from other industrial nations. This is true even in a sector, such as textiles, where the potential challenge is great. Second, there is a requirement for any adjustment assistance that is made available to firms to be orientated towards increased diversification and efficiency rather than to the pure long-term support of employment. Indeed, it has been said that there is no such thing as a declining sector, only declining firms, for efficient and well-managed companies should be moving into new products and technologies on their own accord. Third, policies should assist sectoral adjustments by raising the level and content of local technological change; by improving local management; by encouraging the development of new entrepreneurs and new companies; by improving our understanding of future changes and trends in the international economy; and by educating more people on the needs for and benefits from a more flexible and progressive approach to economic development. Four, it must be accepted that Scotland is a small part of the developed world, and as such has little effective power to fight economic trends. There is a growing understanding of the importance of these factors in economic and industrial policy-making in Scotland, and thus I believe that the longer-term prognosis of the Scottish economy is relatively encouraging.

This brings us to the relationship between Scotland and the Third World. There is much that Scotland can gain from closer links with Third World nations, but incomparably more than we can give to the developing nations. The education and training that is provided is widely recognised and much of the scientific and medical research undertaken in Scotland will have direct benefits overseas. There are also great advantages to be gained commercially through increased links between Scottish and local companies in Third World countries, via joint-ventures, licensing agreements and marketing arrangements, and it is possible to envisage more trade and investment effort being devoted to the Third World countries rather than to North America, Europe and Japan.

Similarly, Scotland, as small nation, shares many of the problems of Third World nations, and thus increased links with countries overseas can help obtain new perspectives on our own development potential, and on our own economic and industrial problems. One such relevant issue concerns the roles that multinational enterprises play in economic development, an issue which has a degree of importance in Scottish economic policy-making.

However, beyond all the above factors remains the fact that the reduction in individual poverty in the Third World remains the single most important policy objective that the world as a whole will have to face in the remaining years of this century. Whilst I would not wish for a moment to avoid the very real problems of poverty and opportunity that remain within Scotland, it must be accepted that those encountered in the Third World are of a totally different magnitude. Reducing these problems will not be easy, and indeed there is no easy agreement about how the relevant development problems can be best tackled. Indeed, it seems probable that the reduction of poverty will require co-ordinated policy action on a wide range of issues, including accelerated industrial development; trade liberalisation; increased real flows of aid and technical assistance; more relevant education; and more efficient agriculture, energy, and health systems.

THE TRADE UNION RESPONSE
TO MULTINATIONALS

by Nigel Howarth

Multinational companies are getting bigger, fewer in number, and more powerful. Today, they produce something like 25% of the gross world product, a larger volume of production than any individual country except the United States. Even the U.S. government has felt the need to examine the growth of multinational power through a series of Congressional hearings,[1] and international agencies like the United Nations, the Organisation for Economic Co-operation and Development (OECD) and the International Labour Organisation (ILO), have deliberated endlessly on the issues raised by the growing influence of multinationals. Codes of conduct have been produced, to be greeted by respectful murmurs of approval from governments, and even nods of acknowledgement from the multinational themselves.

But to what effect? Around the world, hundreds of thousands of workers have learned the hard way, without the need for impressive statistical evidence, that multinational employers are powerful and difficult to control. For all the efforts of governments and international bodies, it is the international trade union movement which has to accept the most direct responsibility for defending the interests of employees against the multinationals.

Over the past ten years, the question of the strategies available to the trade union movement has been moving steadily closer to the centre of debate in union circles. In 1970, Hugh Scanlon referred to the threat of Henry Ford to redirect investment from Britain because of the "intransigence" of British unions, and went on to say that this attitude "graphically illustrates the power of international corporations to ham-string and browbeat the interests of organised labour. We not only need the international labour solidarity to defend our gains, we also need effective control at every stage over the arbitrary power of top management, and effective involvement in every sphere of decision-making."[2]

In contrast to Scanlon's statement, it is rewarding to look at what Frank W. Angle of General Motors says on the issue of international trade unionism:

"The recent drive by certain international trade secretariats in Europe for consultation and bargaining at the international level has a hollow ring in terms of any desire to resolve known conflicts at national and local levels . . . [their] desire to talk to the parent at its headquarters location is merely a disguised attempt to intrude into long-range planning so that the international trade secretariats

can aggrandize their own role in the world trade union movement. .
labour relations is a practical business, and no aspect of it in
General Motors' experience could be improved by the imposition
of international bargaining or consultation with General Motors'
labour-relations management in the home office of the corporation."[3]

In the same vein, an O.E.C.D. study of international labour relations
says:

"Employers were uniformly opposed [to international bargaining]
on the grounds that wages and conditions of work . . . were
determined on the basis of conditions prevailing at the affiliate.
They expressed strong doubts about the capacity of an international union organisation fully to represent the economic interests
of employees in different countries. They also pointed out the
danger that such an organisation would operate outside national
law, and thus be responsible to no-one but itself for its actions."[4]

The two opposing views which emerge from these quotes identify the
issues with which this article is concerned. On the one hand, there is the
desire of workers in MNC's to produce effective responses to the internationalisation of capital embodied in MNC's. On the other hand, there is
the desire of the MNC to contain trade union activity within national
boundaries, and within individual subsidiaries of larger units. As Scanlon
suggests, the issue of control provides the ground for the most basic
confrontation between international capital and the international labour
movement. The international trade union movement, which often faces an
alliance of state and capital, needs to create the analytical and organisational tools with which to control the power of the MNC's.

In this article, I intend to look briefly at the range of strategies currently
being put forward by the international trade union movement, and the
criticisms which they have attracted. I shall conclude by raising a series of
questions not previously considered in the context of workers' offensives
against MNC power.

The Basis of International Trade Unionism

The range of factors governing MNC activities is well documented. The
weight given to the different factors of raw material supply, labour costs,
control of technology, patent laws, market access and political stability in
shaping the location strategy of a particular MNC may vary from company
to company, but the same equation is always buried there somewhere.

There is a popular misconception that MNC's concentrate their activities in the underdeveloped world. But Girvan argues that in 1976, 60% plus of all foreign investment was found in developed economies, and a study of the phases of MNC investment in Scotland tends to confirm this tendency of MNC expansion.[5] This is not, however, to dismiss the importance of the Third World to MNC strategies: indeed, Girvan considers that this relatively low level of investment may be increasingly offset by the high quality of Third World MNC investment.

In the case of Scotland, an added complication arises over the question of whether Scotland should be considered as a developed or an underdeveloped economy, with all the implications that has for any analysis of the nature of investment, production, trade and so on. Whatever conclusions are reached in that debate, the fact remains that approximately 100,000 Scottish jobs are provided by the 140-150 ex-United Kingdom companies which have located their investment here. Indeed, within the United Kingdom, it is Scotland which faces the biggest prospect of change through MNC decision making: thus Scottish trade unionists urgently need to develop coherent and effective strategies towards MNC's.

There are four key dimensions of MNC growth which concern the labour movement:

(a) MNC's and the State

Various forms of contact exist between national governments and MNC's. In the Third World particularly, such contact often takes the form of joint enterprises between state capital and MNC technology and marketing ability. In the developed world, subsidies, tax relief, preferential location terms and a host of other benefits are often offered to MNC's looking for production sites. The British Government's development programme for the "declining" areas aims a whole battery of investment incentives at multinational companies.

Such a close liaison between the state and the MNC's is crucial for several reasons. Firstly, it offers the State a major incentive to intervene in industrial relations practices on the grounds of preserving the conditions which produced the original investment. Secondly, state backing for the MNC may contribute to the ideological impact MNC's have in the regions where they locate their investment. Thirdly, state involvement may legitimise the actions of MNC's in ways which threaten traditional trade union-management relations.

(b) MNC's and Industrial Relations

Whatever the degree of autonomy enjoyed by MNC subsidiaries, MNC's assume a certain minimum of centralised control. In practice, labour relations policy may differ greatly from one MNC subsidiary to another, as the

101

local management adapts to different conditions. But the centralisation of ultimate decision-making power within an MNC does create the possibility of headquarters interference with local collective bargaining relations, personnel practices and recognition of trade union rights, as the Scottish experience illustrates. It should, nevertheless, be acknowledged that many MNC's in Scotland have enjoyed good industrial relations.

(c) MNC's and Local Labour Markets

MNC's have a variety of effects on local labour markets. It is not uncommon for multinationals to pay well above local levels, but the work practices, payment systems and bonus schemes which they operate have to be taken into account, along with the productivity factor, before comparative calculations can be made between MNC wage rates, and those operating within locally-controlled firms.

The implementation of new recruitment policies by MNC's may also affect local labour markets. For example, the arrival of a subsidiary of an MNC which relies on women's labour may change the local recruitment pattern greatly, although this effect is not confined solely to MNC investment. Then there may be a demonstration effect produced in the local labour market by the wage and personnel policies introduced by the newcomer. Workers in local firms may believe that the wages and working conditions in the multinational firm are superior, whatever the reality of the situation. For instance, it is said that the aim of many parents in Greenock is to get their child into IBM (International Business Machines) if at all possible. Where distorted views of job opportunities develop, they may constitute a divisive force within the labour movement.

(d) MNC's and their Effects on Class Formation

As the previous point suggests, the divisions potentially caused by MNC investment in an area can lead to working-class segmentation.

There is the immediate effect on local communities of the implantation of new labour practices and different wage and work systems. The industrial relations practices which stress paternalism, and which are held in high esteem by U.S., Japanese and German companies, have on occasion undermined a traditional trade union base in an area, while the international dimension of the problems produced for a workforce by the very nature of MNC decision-making can lead to a situation in which different issues are preoccupying workers in the national and international sectors. It is possible that the growth of MNC workforces might lead to their constitution as a distinct fragment of the working class, so undermining the potential for inter-firm action or solidarity.

While one can readily identify these dimensions of the impact of MNC investment, it is not so easy to establish the basis for future trade union unity across organisational and national boundaries. Olle and Schoeller make the important point that there is no *necessary* logic whereby because MNC's expand across national boundaries, and operate as international units, the trade union movement will automatically follow suit.[6] The internationalisation of the labour movement will be the product of political and organisational reform, challenging the existing basis of national and international trade union organisations, and creating qualitatively new forces properly equipped for the conflict with the new forms of international capital.

Olle and Schoeller suggest that the existing international strategy of the trade union movement accepts that the objective circumstances for the internationalisation of the trade union movement have been produced by the internationalisation of capital. In this orthodox view, all that is required to consolidate an international trade union response is the building of an appropriate 'politico-legal' structure for the trade union movement. This approach results in the trade union movement merely responding to the actions of international capital, never initiating action. This "tail-ending" approach is reinforced by the fact that the strategy emerges from the existing institutions of the labour movement, and generally does not challenge the viability of what are really at present national trade union institutions, stretched to constitute international institutions.

One can see these problems clearly when one identifies the basic components of the existing orthodox trade union strategy, as expressed by both British and international activists within the labour movement. There are six broad strands to the trade union response to the MNC threat.

(a) The Demand for Unity

There are constant demands for the development of international links between workers in a particular MNC, and between workers in particular industrial sectors. Hughes believes that this unity must be forged on the basis of well-funded and co-ordinated activity, and suggests that the formal institutions of the labour movement are adequate to achieve this unity.[7] The T.U.C. is suggested as the body around which international co-operation and strategy should revolve insofar as it affects British worker organisations. The French union C.G.T (Confédération General du Travail) stresses the role of education and information in the building of unity between workers in particular MNC's.

(b) Restructuring the International Trade Union Institutions

It is generally agreed by trade union writers that the existing trade union structures will require major reforms if the trade union movement is to respond effectively to the MNC threat. In the British case, Hughes sees the impetus for reform coming from the T.U.C., while also identifying a need for organisational reforms stretching down to the shop floor. Bye and Usher point to the growth of the European T.U.C. as an important stage in the development of new labour organisations, and welcomes the emergence of international trade secretariats, of which there are now sixteen. The types of long-term contacts set up by, for example, the Dunlop-Pirelli workers also allows some commentators to believe that there is evolving a new level of international union organisation.

(c) The Gathering of Information

The timely provision of information is seen as crucial, never more so than in the case of mergers involving rationalisation of jobs and plants. Gennard makes the point, to which further attention will be given, that the usefulness of information is greatly increased by its being available before the events it concerns are brought about by the MNC. This emphasis on the advantages of anticipation is echoed by the French C.G.T.

(d) International Controls over MNC's

When it comes to tackling the investment and locational strategies of the MNC's, most followers of the orthodox view of international trade union strategy believe that national governments and supranational institutions have the greatest potential for countervailing action. The International Confederation of Free Trade Unions (I.C.F.T.U.), to which the British T.U.C. is affiliated, calls for the U.N. and the E.E.C. to institute coherent control policies over MNC activities, while the I.L.O. and the O.E.C.D. have placed their faith in international codes of conduct, setting out the ground rules for "reasonable" MNC behaviour. This emphasis on the effects of international legislation and pressure is reflected in the British T.U.C.'s call for international control over MNC's, with a particular reference to the need for MNC's to recognise international norms in respect of union recognition and rights.

(e) MNC's and Public Accountability

It is generally agreed that MNC's should be made publicly accountable. Hughes argues that the former U.K. Prices and Incomes Board and the Monopoly Commission supply skeleton models of effective control agencies for dealing with MNC's. Particularly significant was their power to impose national legislation on MNC's, legislation which might be adapted to incorporate policies to meet the shifts of MNC strategy. As Scanlon and others have indicated, one crucial issue in the move to make MNC's publicly accountable would be to enforce the call to "open the books" in a way which undermined MNC manoeuvres to avoid the disclosure of information. Public accountability might also be fostered through the effects of worker participation schemes (such as that proposed for MNC subsidiaries in Britain by the Bullock Report), or by the imposition of workers' control.

(f) Labour Movement Involvement in MNC Planning

Scanlon argues that the best long-term hope for trade union control over

MNC's rests in union involvement in the planning of MNC policy. Suggested forms of trade union involvement include workers' control, planning agreements, industrial participation and forms of joint consultation at various levels, from individual plant to national government. It is argued for all of these strategies that they are as applicable at an international level as at the level of a national trade union movement. However, most of these suggestions are highly generalised, and the failure of the Chrysler planning agreement (see the essay by Neil Hood and Stephen Young in this volume) reminds us that successes in this area are rare.

Problems with the Orthodox Strategy

One can identify four major problems which hinder the implementation of the orthodox international trade union strategy, each of which can be traced back to the underlying assumption that the internationalisation of capital generates the basis for a reflexive international trade unionism. The identification of these problems leads to a consideration of the changes necessary to overcome them.

(a) The Continuing Lack of Organisational and Informational Activity

Despite valiant efforts by formal and informal sections of the labour movement, and the emergence of organisations such as the European T.U.C., it must be accepted that both at the level of information flow and the level of organisation, the union movement still trails far behind the MNC's in organisational capacity. Despite attempts to co-ordinate activities, strategy is still formulated piecemeal at all levels of the trade union movement. Important international decisions are being left to bodies which are remote from the rank-and-file worker in the MNC, and information—the key to any activity within an MNC—is usually gathered either haphazardly, or through the individual efforts of committed conveners and stewards. Union officials charged with MNC responsibility are stretched beyond the point where they can give efficient service to plant branches or wider organisations. If national and international co-ordination is to be developed, a new theory of multinational labour activity and new organisations are both required.

(b) Tail-Ending Forever

It is a common complaint of activists in the labour movement that the trade unions are always "tail-ending" the decisions of MNC's. The complaint is justified. Typically, the trade unions' role in relation to MNC's is reactive: not until the MNC reveals its own strategy do the unions begin their planning. As the MNC's are naturally secretive about their strategy, this forces the unions into hasty and confused responses which the MNC managements are often able to neutralise.

The trade unions urgently need to equip themselves with the professional and technical expertise to carry out their own forward analysis of MNC strategy, and to improve their means of disseminating information.

(c) The Negative Response Syndrome
Because the issues over which MNC's and unions confront each other have typically been identified by management initiatives, rather than those of the trade unions, there is an in-built tendency for union responses to take a defensive form.

State intervention is often called for when it is clear even to the unions that this *in itself* cannot provide the solution to redundancies, major disinvestment and so on. Straightforward demands to maintain production in a threatened plant, or to introduce a new product, may lack credibility in the face of the management's greater experience of the market possibilities. What is needed on the union side is an *offensive* argument which seeks to replace the MNC's definition of the problem with a union definition. Of course the unions must be able to present an effective critique of the MNC's case in its own terms, but they also need to offer alternative standards of judgement based on the needs of the labour force or of the wider society. An offensive strategy of this sort would, again, require higher levels of information, analysis and planning than most unions are able to offer at present— co-ordinated and presented, moreover, in the framework of an "alternative plan".

(d) The Institutionalisation of Trade Union Responses
There is a noticeable tendency for union responses to MNC's to become institutionally distanced from the people most directly affected by MNC initiatives. Formal union channels are at present the most developed means of international union communication, but these are remote from the normal shop-floor worker. Although several well-documented cases do exist of British unionists forming informal links internationally ("Newhaven-Dieppe" workers, Massey workers in Scotland and France) while still making use of the available formal channels, informal links have not yet been properly developed. Informal inter-union, inter-combine contacts within MNC's provide an indispensable complement to the formal organisations at both national and international levels. There are problems associated with the formation of such links, but these are not insuperable, and there is no doubt that the extension of such links would greatly increase the cohesion of the international trade union movement.

To summarise: there is a growing recognition among trade unionists of the need to develop new strategies to face up to MNC's. This recognition embraces a belief that the existing trade union institutions are inadequate, not because of deliberate manipulation by trade union bureaucrats or Machiavellian management, but because trade union strategists have failed to make an adequate appreciation of the new challenge created by the growth in MNC power. What remedies are available to the international trade union movement?

Towards a Strategy

The remedies should be sought in changes to the existing structures which determine the labour movement's response to MNC's, and in different emphases in trade union activity. The British labour movement has two broad options as it attempts to develop international labour solidarity to meet the challenge of international capital. Firstly, the existing formal structures within the labour movement—International Trade Secretariats, E.T.U.C., I.C.F.T.U. etc—could be reinforced, and their scope of activity extended. Both at T.U.C. level, and at individual union level, international contacts could be strengthened through the provision of better facilities for the international sections of these organisations. Information flows could be developed by the creation of research directorates with wider powers and better funding than at present both at national and international level. The educational function of the formal organisations could be extended to produce and disseminate information about MNC's which at present is not easily available to the mass of union members. This is particularly relevant in the case of information about the dependent economies of the under-developed world. State-level interventions are not easily handled within the formal structures, but if they are to take their place in a coherent inter-national strategy they need to be far better co-ordinated. Few of these points will be disputed within the United Kingdom or abroad.

Secondly, new attitudes and new activities are required within the labour movement to provide the positive, offensive function identified earlier. In developing an offensive strategy, emphasis should be placed on two inter-connected needs now becoming increasingly important to the U.K. labour movement. Firstly, the formation of national, and eventually international labour combines in MNC's is an essential prerequisite if the unity to support an offensive strategy is to be created. Such combines can contribute significantly to the combativity of the labour force in large organisations. The inter-plant contact made possible by the formation of combines en-courages a wider and more comprehensive flow of information, which is also advanced in practice by an observable unity between the work-force and the professionals in information provision, which is a fairly new character-istic of labour activity. The solidarity which characterises a combine derives from the perception of a common interest binding together the labour force in different plants belonging to the same firm. This is something which general union activity cannot hope to duplicate, and this kind of solidarity supplies its own impetus towards a better flow of information. The infor-mation gathered is specific to the MNC, and is more easily translated into international activity within the MNC because of its *direct* relevance. Henry Friedman has outlined the issues involved in combine formation, and the recent experience of the major combines operating (Vickers, Lucas, G.E.C., I.C.I. etc.) has shown the positive contribution they can make to unity in particular enterprises.[8]

Secondly the question of 'alternative planning strategy' takes on a vital role in conjunction with the growth of MNC combines. The Lucas plan has attracted a great deal of attention, and some have rejected it out of hand as playing into the hands of capital, trying to do its job for it. This negative response seems to come from two sources.

The first is the belief that alternative planning is "playing capital's game", hence a deviation from the path of true socialism. The adherents of this position have to admit that much of what even they themselves call for does not lead to socialism *in itself*, and that it is important to engage in activities which can mobilise, organise and educate, and which include notions of *involvement* in the formulation of strategy. Alternative planning which derives from the labour force, and which challenges management authority, is progressive because it mobilises people around important issues concerning power, control and the purpose of production under capitalism.

The second objection arises from the fear that alternative planning will undermine the traditional institutions and strategies of the labour movement. But this position has to face the evident limitations of the traditional structures of the labour movement in taking on international capital. Any development which promotes unity and international co-operation must be given its chance, and not dismissed just because it is not in the image of previous activities.

Alternative planning offers clear advantages to the international labour movement. Firstly, the production of an alternative plan requires a high degree of mobilisation and commitment in a labour force, and can help consolidate inter-plant activities. Hence the central role of the combine in this approach. Alternative planning can also provide a focus which allows wider issues to be brought into discussions, as the narrow horizons on the single plant are discarded. Secondly, the development of an alternative plan can transfer the management-labour clash on to ground at least partially defined by the labour force. This is because alternative plans offer the possibility of avoiding the situation in which union actions are always developed as a response to management decisions. Alternative planning has the power not only to undermine management proposals by counterposing a coherent plan devised by the workforce: it can also bring the issue of the social effects of production to the fore. Alternative plans pose socially-relevant production against production for profit in the market. The importance of this can hardly be overestimated, because it represents a break in the tradition whereby management and labour have accepted production-for-profit as the basis for industrial organisation. Workers' control is a natural

108

extension of this line of argument, wherein production is determined socially by the producers, with market criteria being rejected as the basis for production decision-making. Alternative plans do not in themselves bring about socialism, but they do at least raise the issues of how socialist production might be ordered, and how a transition to it might be achieved. Finally, alternative plans allow a labour force to acquire skills previously denied to them by the division of labour in production as it presently exists. The divorce of the planning function from the production function evident in capitalist production can be overcome by the involvement of a workforce in the production of an alternative plan, thereby demystifying the decision-making process.

The importance of parallel combine development to the creation of alternative plans can readily be seen. The unity and co-ordination of a combine is crucial in terms of information flow and policy formulation for alternative plans, whilst the alternative plan undermines the "tail-ending" nature of union responses, and offers an offensive strategy to the labour movement. The adoption of an offensive strategy becomes ever more important as MNC power develops.

As Scotland's experience of the Linwood saga demonstrates, the labour movement cannot depend on the state to provide the answer. The answer must come from the movement itself. Through the development of alternative plans and of combines, and the adaptation of existing formal organisations, the labour movement can devise an effective response to the multinational challenge outlined by Hugh Scanlon more than a decade ago.

References

1. See, for example, U.S. Congress Joint Economic Committee, Hearings, *A Foreign Economic Policy for the 1970s, Part 4, Multinational Corporations and International Investment,* U.S. Government 1970.

2. H. Scanlon *Workers' Control and the Threat of the Multinational Companies* Trade Union Register 1970   Martin 1970.

3. F.W. Angle *The Conduct of Labour Relations in General Motors' Overseas Operations,* in D. Kujawa (ed) *International Labour and the Multinational Enterprise*   Praeger 1975.

4. OECD *The Industrial Relations and Employment Impacts of Multinational Enterprises* by A. Morgan and R. Blainpain 1977.

5. N. Girvan *Corporate Imperialism: Conflict and Expropriation* Monthly Review Press 1976.

6. W. Olle and W. Schoeller *World Market Competition and Restrictions upon International Trade Union Policies.* Capital and Class No. 2.

7. J. Hughes 'Giant Firms and British Trade Unions' Response' *Trade Union Register 1970*   Martin 1970.

8. H. Friedman *Multi-plant Working and Trade Union Organisation* Workers Educational Association.

DEPENDENT INDUSTRIALIZATION
IN THE THIRD WORLD

by Rhys Jenkins

1. Introduction

Eight years ago in a controversial article in the *New Left Review,* Bill Warren argued that contrary to the generally held view on the Left, substantial capitalist development had taken place in the Third World since World War II and that this could be characterized as independent industrialization! More specifically Warren attacked the view put forward by Bob Sutcliffe, among others, that imperialism is an obstacle to independent industrialization in the underdeveloped areas.² In view of Warren's attack on the whole concept of dependent industrialization, it is necessary first to justify the use of the term at all.

Sutcliffe identified conditions which must be satisfied for industrialization to qualify as 'independent'. Industrialization must

(i) be based primarily on the home market

(ii) incorporate local production of a wide range of industries including economically strategic capital goods

(iii) not be under the direct control of foreign capital

(iv) be based on independent technological progress.

One of the principal exponents of "underdevelopment theory", Samir Amin, has something similar in mind when he draws a distinction between the self-centred system of capital accumulation of the advanced countries and that of the peripheral countries.³ The former is based on the dynamic relationship between production of mass consumption goods and capital goods, whereas the latter depends on production for export which creates a demand in the underdeveloped countries for local manufacture of certain luxury consumer goods. Peripheral dependent industrialization is therefore characterized by a relative expansion of luxury good production controlled by multinational corporations (MNC's) and a lack of development of both basic consumer goods and capital goods accompanied by a technological gap with respect to the developed countries.

Warren points out quite correctly that industrial output has grown rapidly in many underdeveloped countries (UDC's) in the post-war period and that in most cases this has been based on import substitution for the domestic market (although as we shall see later there are a number of important

111

exceptions). He is less convincing when he argues that a wide range of industries have been developed, including crucially the capital goods industries. While it is true that the more advanced UDC's have developed a number of intermediate industries such as iron and steel and chemicals, and even some capital goods industries, they still depend heavily on imported machinery and equipment from the advanced countries. In five countries studied by OECD in the 1960's imports of capital goods were a substantial share of total supplies in all except Brazil. In India more than 40% of capital goods were imported and in Mexico, Pakistan and the Phillippines around 60%.[4] Since these include four of the five largest UDC's in terms of GNP, and are therefore likely to enjoy particularly favourable conditions for the development of a capital goods industry, it can be seen that other countries depend to an even greater extent on imports. Nevertheless this situation is changing and it is becoming increasingly difficult to argue that imperialism poses an insurmountable obstacle to the development of capital goods industries in the Third World.

Warren also argues that foreign financing is relatively unimportant, with direct foreign investment accounting for only about 5% of total fixed capital formation in the under-developed countries. Contrary to Warren's view that this reflects a high level of independence for these countries, I would maintain that they reflect certain financial strategies of the MNC's which raise funds locally and re-invest locally made profits rather than transferring capital from the parent company. This is the only way in which one can reconcile the low volume of capital inflows to developing countries with the high share, of a third or more, of manufacturing sales or assets controlled by MNC's.

Finally Warren's position is least convincing regarding independent technological progress, which he regards as occurring virtually automatically with the development of a capital goods industry. He fails to recognise that there is a real difference between the ability to operate an established plant producing capital goods in a national economy and the ability to innovate in terms of products, production processes and plant design. The identification of technology with hardware in the form of a capital goods industry serves only to fudge the issues.

Nevertheless Warren's article performed an important function by challenging a number of assumptions which had become virtually articles of faith among radical writers on underdevelopment. In some cases there had been a tendency to argue that since development was not benefitting the masses, then development was not taking place at all, conveniently forgetting that the purpose of capitalist development had never been to benefit the masses. It followed logically therefore that since socialist development did not occur under capitalism, the only solution was socialism!

Dependent Industrialization in the Third World

Capitalist industrialization in the Third World does however differ from the pattern set by the advanced countries and the term "dependent industrialization" is a useful one for bringing out this difference. In the rest of this paper I shall discuss some of the features of the two characteristic forms taken by Third World industrialization, import substitution and export promotion.

2. Import substituting industrialization (ISI)

ISI has been the dominant pattern of industrialization in the Third World in the post-war period. Pioneered by the Latin American countries and some of the larger Asian countries like India and Pakistan, it has been followed more recently by other Asian and African countries. First prompted in Latin America by the economic crisis of the inter-war period, it consisted of producing locally, behind protective barriers, commodities that had previously been imported. It led to a substantial widening of the spectrum of industrial production to include luxury consumer goods such as cars, televisions and refrigerators and intermediate goods such as chemicals, rubber, and iron and steel.

The proponents of ISI held out great hopes for this strategy of development, comparing it to the use of tariffs in the nineteenth century by Germany and the United States as part of their strategy to catch up with the world industrial leader, Britain. ISI was regarded as a break with the traditional role of the UDC's as suppliers of primary products to the developed countries. It would permit goods to be produced locally thus generating additional employment. It was even argued by some that it would lead to political democratization by shifting power away from feudal oligarchies.

What was not envisaged by the advocates of import substitution was the way in which it was to lead to the dominance of multinational corporations in the new industries created, through direct investment and licensing agreements. These companies, seeing their traditional export markets threatened by attempts to create a local industry, set up manufacturing plants in the underdeveloped countries. As a result they increased their share of manufacturing production rapidly. This is best documented in Latin America where the participation of foreign companies increased by more than 60% in Argentina between 1959 and 1972[5] and by more than 40% in Mexico between 1962 and 1970.[6] In Brazil, United States owned MNC's increased their share of manufacturing sales by more than a half in only four years between 1966 and 1970.[7]

Typically MNC's control directly between a third and a half of industrial production in the main Latin American countries. In certain industries.

such as rubber, chemicals, pharmaceuticals, electrical equipment and vehicles they have much higher shares. They also account for a disproportionately large share of the output of the largest companies in each country. In both Argentina and Brazil MNC's accounted for around 60% of the sales of the largest 100 companies in 1972. In Mexico such firms were responsible for more than half the sales of the largest 189 industrial companies in 1974.[9] Moreover these figures do not include locally owned firms that operate under licence from MNC's which also figure prominently among the largest industrial firms.

This increasing penetration of the underdeveloped countries' industry by the multinationals has been a major criticism levelled at import substitution by the so-called "dependency theorists". They point out that far from reducing dependence on the international economy, import substitution has merely created a new form of dependence. In place of dependence on world markets for primary products and on a few MNC's in resource-based industries, the new dependence involves foreign control of manufacturing, imports of intermediate and capital goods and increasing payment of dividends, royalties and interest to foreign capital.

There is however a tendency to see foreign control of manufacturing industry as a "bad thing" in its own right, thus avoiding the need to specify the adverse consequences of the absence of national control. While foreign ownership in itself may be objectionable from a nationalistic standpoint it is not enough simply to assert that it constitutes an obstacle to development. This rightly provokes the response from critics both of the right and the left that MNC's respond to market conditions, factor prices, etc., and must be shown to behave differently from nationally controlled capital.

Different conditions are found in different industries where production has become internationalized and here I shall try to illustrate the specific mechanisms of dependence by considering the operations of three industries in the underdeveloped countries. These industries are pharmaceuticals, cars and electrical equipment, all of which have seen substantial internationalization of production in the post-war period.

The pharmaceutical industry is one of the most highly international in the world. The major US laboratories e.g. Johnson and Johnson, American Home Products, Warner Lambert and Bristol Myers sell between a third and a half of their output overseas, while for Swiss laboratories such as Ciba-Geigy, Hoffman La Roche and Sandoz the proportion is over 90%. A large part of these overseas sales are made by manufacturing affiliates of which the major US companies had over 300 in 1968 and the non-US multinationals over 200 in 1971.[10] The major cause of this internationalization of production in the industry is the very high level of research and development expenditure which accounts for 10% or more of the turnover of the large pharmaceutical companies. It is in the interest of the companies to spread these costs over the largest possible volume of sales and one way of doing this is to expand into overseas markets. Because the final stage of pharmaceutical production, dosage form fabrication, is relatively simple and labour-intensive the MNC's have transferred this stage to the UDC's often supplying the raw material (active ingredients) from the parent company.

The pharmaceutical industry is highly profitable internationally, earning rates of return well above the average for manufacturing as a whole. These profits are derived from the barriers to entry to the industry caused by the large amounts of capital required for research and development, patent protection and high levels of spending on marketing. In the advanced countries where these firms have their headquarters and research laboratories, these profits are partly reinvested in research and development. In the underdeveloped countries, however, little is spent on R and D while profits are correspondingly even higher.

One of the most important consequences of the structure of the international pharmaceutical industry for the developing countries has been the pricing behaviour of the major companies. The industry has become notorious for the way in which it uses transfer pricing (i.e. arbitrary internal company prices) in order to shift funds between countries. Although this has been used against developed countries as in the case of Hoffman La Roche in Britain, it has been felt most severely in the Third World. Various studies have shown over-pricing of intermediate products in the industry by up to 40 or 50 times.[11] This enables the companies to avoid declaring profits and being taxed in the UDC's. A number of MNC's in the industry have gone so far as to locate some production facilities in tax havens such as the Bahamas and the Republic of Ireland. Thus in order to minimise their total tax burden they have an interest in not declaring profits in the UDC's.

The motor industry is also highly internationalized in terms both of production and of sales and the 1960's and 1970's have seen a substantial increase in assembly and manufacturing operations in the Third World. The industry is also highly concentrated at the international level with four firms accounting for more than half of world production and thirteen companies for almost 90%. This high level of concentration has been associated with intense oligopolistic rivalry in order to enter new markets. The leading MNC's in the industry have played "follow-my-leader" whenever one of their number has been induced to set up in a particular UDC. As a result the characteristic feature of the industry in the Third World has been the fragmentation of small national markets between a large number of foreign subsidiaries. Since there is no relation between market size relative to the optimum scale of plant and the decision of the MNC's to set up local operations the result is a proliferation of small, high cost production units. The problem is aggravated by the marketing strategies of the companies which emphasize model diversity and model changes thus reducing the production runs for any particular model.

In contrast to the situation in the advanced industrial countries where an initially large number of firms in the motor industry was reduced to a handful through bankruptcies and mergers, there is little possibility of this occuring in UDC markets dominated by MNC's. Even the largest UDC market only represents a small part of the total operation of a MNC and a presence could be maintained in the face of local losses for a long period of time. Since all the subsidiaries are in the same position, there is no incentive to attempt to overcome the problems of small scale production through intense competition for market shares. A policy of live and let live with high costs and high prices is in the interest of all firms. This, of course, serves to limit the expansion of the market and the accumulation of capital in the industry.

The third sector which I wish to consider briefly is the electrical industry. This includes capital goods such as turbines, transformers and switchgear, and consumer goods such as radios, televisions and record players. The industry internationally is highly concentrated with firms such as GE and Westinghouse in the USA, GEC in Britain, Siemens and AEG in Germany and Hitachi in Japan producing a whole range of products while other firms like Philips (consumer products) and Brown Boveri (heavy electrical equipment) concentrate on particular lines. Aggregate data on concentration internationally is difficult to get but concentration appears to be higher in capital goods than in consumer products. The major MNC's in the industry have at least a quarter of their sales overseas with important foreign manufacturing subsidiaries. The major companies internationally are linked to each other through equity holdings, joint ventures and cross licensing arrangements which all serve to increase oligopolistic interdependence in the industry.

The electrical industry has a long history of collusive behaviour and restrictive practices. Market allocation arrangements between the leading producers before World War II retarded the development of the industry in many UDC's. There seemed to be a tacit recognition that the Third World should remain an importer from the advanced countries. When after the war the threat of local production in some UDC's led the electrical MNC's to set up foreign subsidiaries marked spheres of influence were maintained. It had been suggested that US MNC's concentrated on Central America, Spanish South America and the Phillippines, while the non-US firms concentrated on Southern Europe and Africa. These territorial divisions of world markets reduced competition and undoubtedly raised prices and profits in the industry. The high price of imported heavy electrical equipment transfers income to the MNC's in the developed countries and, since such equipment is an important element in investment, tends to reduce the real rate of accumulation within the UDC's. The restrictive business practices and use of economic power by the MNC's prevents new competitors from emerging in the underdeveloped countries. They have also prevented vertical integration in many cases, for example forward into the cable industry by the major copper exporting countries, or backwards into parts and components.[12]

3. World-wide sourcing

A second kind of manufacturing operation which has expanded substantially in a number of UDC's in recent years involves investment to take advantage of the cheap labour of these areas in order to export to the advanced industrial countries. Hong Kong, Singapore, Taiwan and South Korea pioneered this type of industrialization in the 1960s but more recently it has been extended to a number of other developing countries. This is frequently associated with free production zones where firms are allowed to import parts, materials and capital goods free of duty, granted tax holidays and provided with buildings and other facilities. In the mid-1970s such zones were in operation in twenty-five UDC's and under construction in a further eleven. They employed an estimated half a million workers.[13]

It is necessary to see this phenomenon in the context of certain recent developments in world capitalism. It has been made possible by the development of the forces of production in transport and communications such as the introduction of jet aircraft, containerization, telex and international telephone services which have tended to free industrial location from proximity to markets. It has also resulted from the development of the labour process within manufacturing generally which has involved an increasing division of labour in detail within the factory and a consequent deskilling of the mass of workers. This makes it possible to fragment the production process and relocate parts of it which require large number of cheap, undifferentiated and untrained workers in the Third World.

The tendency for "world-wide sourcing" becomes increasingly important from about the mid-1960s. It coincides with the exhaustion of the reserve army in most of the advanced capitalist countries which had been replenished during two decades of post-war boom through the use of immigrant labour in Europe, the incorporation of the peasantry in Italy and Japan and the incorporation of women, particularly in the USA. In the Mid-1960s the rate of surplus value in the developed countries began to decline as the balance of forces shifted in favour of the working class to produce a substantial increase in real wages and profit rates began to fall. Certain sectors, particularly electrical products and clothing where labour-intensive production processes were important, began to relocate these processes in the UDC's This was most pronounced in the United States where wage rates were highest and Japan where they had been increasing rapidly.

Dependent Industrialization in the Third World

A crucial factor in the transfer of these operations to the Third World is the availability of a suitable labour force in these areas. It has been found that in export processing, wages in UDC's are anywhere from one twentieth to a fifth of wages in equivalent jobs in the United States. Unskilled wage rates of between £0.15 and £0.25 an hour were found in many countries in the mid-1970s. In contrast the studies of the United States Tariff Commission concluded:

> "the productivity of workers in foreign establishments assembling or processing products of United States origin generally approximates that of workers of the same job classification in the United States."[14]

The combination of far lower wages and almost equal productivity results in huge differences in labour costs per unit of output.

Low wage levels are maintained because of the large reserve army of labour existing in the UDC's and the relatively low level of union organization. In Hong Kong only 6.5% of the industrial labour force was unionized while in the Mexican border industry unionization was weak or non-existent.[15] This is reflected in a low incidence of industrial disputes in countries such as South Korea, Singapore and Taiwan. Indeed in advertising their facilities these countries emphasise the docility of their labour force.

Hours of work in manufacturing in the UDC's are often extremely long. In South Korea 60 hours a week is normal in the export industries and in some cases the working week consists of seven twelve hour days. In Hong Kong more than half the labour force work 10 hours or more a day and more than half work 7 days a week. In Singapore working days of ten to twelve hours are common.[16]

All these tendencies are intensified by the predominant use of female labour in Third World export production. Young women aged between 15 and 25 account for more than 70% of employment. They are paid wages which are between 20% and 50% of those earned by men. They also tend to be less organized than male workers and to constitute a less stable labour force. Typically labour turnover is high, reaching levels of 50% a year, but this is no great disadvantage for the firms since the need for training is minimal and it fits in with a hiring and firing policy which seeks to impede worker organization.

It is worth noting here that exports of manufactured goods have increasingly come to be regarded by economists and international organizations such as the OECD as the most viable development strategy for Third World countries. Taiwan and South Korea are frequently held up as shining examples of what can be achieved in this field. It is argued that a greater adherence to the principles of comparative advantage and therefore an emphasis on exports of labour-intensive products will resolve many of the problems which have arisen with import substitution. Not only will it help to improve the balance of payments situation but it will also generate higher levels of employment to absorb the rapidly growing labour force.

The model involves increased levels of integration with the advanced capitalist countries and it may be no coincidence that the countries which have taken the lead in this field (Hong Kong, Singapore, Taiwan and South Korea, especially the last two) also have a direct political interest in such integration. However as a development strategy for the Third World as a whole it raises a number of questions. As already mentioned, an increasing number of UDC's are entering the field of manufactured exports, and competition within the sectors which have become internationalized in this way is likely to intensify. Increasing competition between UDC's to attract this kind of investment is likely to reduce the share of the benefits appropriated by the producing country, while increased production is likely to reduce prices and therefore the total value in which they share. Once one gets away from simplistic notions of the terms of trade being a result of peculiar characteristics of certain products, it becomes clear that specialization in labour-intensive manufactures may differ little from specialization in primary products.

This type of export production is characterized by its footlooseness which makes it possible to shift from one low cost location to another at short notice. Production involves very limited capital equipment. Physical facilities are frequently provided by the local government in return for a rent. Because the training of workers is minimal, the costs of moving to a new location are extremely low. In the Mexican border industries employment fell by a third in the first half of 1975 with 26,000 workers being laid off. In Mauritius there were a number of plant closures in the export processing zone in the past couple of years with a loss of more than a thousand jobs. As a long-run strategy therefore export production is characterized by a significant element of uncertainty.

It is unlikely to have the employment creating effects attributed to it by its main advocates. Although in a few small economies with populations of a few million it does offer an opportunity to make an impact on the unemployment problem, for the Third World as a whole there is no possibility of this occurring. Countries such as Brazil and India would require astronomical increases in their exports in order to make a dent in the employment problem.[18]

The other side of the coin of this transfer of production processes to the UDC's is the effect on labour in the developed countries. Up to now worldwide sourcing has not advanced as far in Britain and Europe as it has in the United States and Japan so that the impact on the working class has been relatively limited, but this is no guarantee that Britain will not follow in the footsteps of these countries in the foreseeable future. The sectors in which this process has mainly been concentrated—clothing, electronics and some light manufactures—have traditionally been sectors in which the weakest sections of the working class have been found, namely women and to some extent immigrants. Resistance to the trend has therefore been relatively weak so far. However if world-wide sourcing continues to expand at current rates, increased conflicts are likely to arise.

The emerging pattern appears to be for MNC's in the developed countries to favour free trade which permits them to import from subsidiaries in cheap labour countries. Firms which have not internationalized tend to join labour in calling for protection. However the contradiction that arises here is that protection to preserve jobs prevents industry from increasing productivity. On the other hand workers quite rightly feel that in the absence of protection, jobs are bound to be lost and there is no guarantee that they will be reemployed in new higher productivity jobs. Moreover there is no guarantee that protection will in the long run preserve jobs. Capital may in fact use the profits earned behind tariff barriers in order to diversify out of the protected industry into a new product which generates far less employment, as happened with the Dundee jute industry.

Conclusion

The integration of the underdeveloped countries into the international economy has affected them in different ways depending on the particular sector being considered and the type of industrialization (import substitution or export oriented). The MNC's have much greater freedom to avoid controls and shift funds out of underdeveloped countries, through transfer pricing, for example than have locally owned firms. Moreover in research intensive industries such as pharmaceuticals they need to transfer surplus to the parent company since the key area for the expansion of capital is continuous research and development, which is located in the developed countries. In other industries oligopolistic structures in the international markets have led either to high costs and high prices (cars) or high profits and high prices (electrical equipment). In manufacturing export industries, production is based on cheap and unorganized labour, usually female, with minimal effects on the host economy apart from the actual employment generated. In aggregate this has done little to resolve the employment problem in the Third World and its popularity as a development strategy probably reflects the interest of the MNC's in cheap labour.

1. Warren, B., "Imperialism and Capitalist Industrialization", *NLR* 81. 1973.

2. Sutcliffe, B., "Imperialism and Industrialisation in the Third World"

in R. Owen and B. Sutcliffe, *Studies in the Theory of Imperialism* London, Longman. 1972.

3. Amin, S., "Accumulation and Development: a theoretical model." *Review of African Political Economy*, No. 1. 1974.

4. Little, I., Scitovsky, T. and Scott, M., *Industry and Trade in some Developing Countries,* Oxford University Press for OECD. 1970

5. Sourrouille, J., *The Impact of Transnational Enterprises or Employment and Income: The Case of Argentina*, Geneva, ILO, World Employment Programme WEP 2-28/WP 7. 1976.

6. Sepulveda, B. and Chumacero, A., *La Inversion Extranjera en Mexico,* Mexico City, Fondo de Cultura Economica, 1973.

7. Newfarmer, R. and Meuller, W., *Multinational Corporations in Brazil and Mexico. Structural Sources of Economic and Non-economic Power.* Report to the subcommittee on Multinational Corporations of the Committee on Foreign Relations, United States Senate, Washington, U.S. Government Printing Office. 1975.

8. Chapoy Bonifaz, A., *Empresas Multinacionales,* Mexico City, Ediciones "El Caballito". 1975.

9. Jenkins, R.O., *Transnational Corporations and their Impact on the Mexican Economy*, Development Studies Discussion Paper No. 43. 1978.

10. Vaupel, J.W. and Curhan, J.P., *The World's Multinational Enterprises: A sourcebook of tables based on a study of the largest U.S. and non-U.S. manufacturing corporations,* Geneva, Centre for Education in International Management. 1973.

11. UNCTAD, *Major issues in Transfer of Technology to Developing Countries: As Case Study of the Pharmaceutical Industry*, UN. TD/B/C.6/4. 1975.

12. Newfarmer, R., *Multinational Conglomerates and the Economics of Dependent Development*. Ph.D. Thesis, University of Wisconsin-Madison. 1977.

13. Frank, A.G., *Third World Manufacturing Export Production,* Development Studies Discussion Paper No. 37. 1979.

14. U.S. Tariff Commission, *Economic Factors Affecting the use of items*

807.00 and 806.30 of the Tariff Schedules of the U.S., Washington. 1970.

15. Trajtenberg, R., *Transnational Enterprises and the Cheap Labour Force in Less Developed Countries,* Geneva, ILO, World Employment Programme, WEP 2128/WP.15. 1976.

16. Frank, A.G., *Superexploitation in the Third World,* Development Studies Reprint, No. 64. 1978. pp. 19-20.

17. Frank, A.G., ibid p.10.

18. Tyler, W., "Manufactured Exports and Employment Creation in Developing Countries: Some Empirical Evidence," *Economic Development and Cultural Change.*

THE LINWOOD EXPERIENCE: CHRYSLER AND PEUGEOT-CITROEN IN SCOTLAND

by Stephen Young and Neil Hood

Introduction

It is probably true that as much public attention has been focussed on the foreign-owned Linwood car plant in Scotland as on all the other two hundred or so multinational (MNE) affiliates operating in the country combined. This partly reflects the fact that while in the late 1950s Singer at Clydebank had employed as many as 15,000 people and NCR at a maximum in 1969/70 employed 6,500 personnel in Dundee, these operations suffered major job rundowns in the 1970s, leading in the case of the Singer plant to closure. Together they provided employment for only about 3000 people as the 1970s decade ended.[1] By comparison, although employment at Linwood fluctuated widely, the plant employed 7500 people in 1979 and still nearly 5000 in early 1981. Chrysler and Peugeot-Citroen were thus highly visible in Scotland.

The reasons for the constant glare of publicity surrounding the operations go much further than mere size. Linwood was the only car factory in Scotland, and when the Hillman Imp began to roll off the production line in May 1963 this was the first Scottish-produced car since 1928. The location of the manufacturing facilities has also contributed. The economic and social problems of Clydeside have been and remain particularly severe. Linwood was in a position, therefore, where it could partially alleviate these difficulties.

Overrriding all of these factors were the more general problems of foreign ownership. Since Chrysler first took a minority shareholding in Rootes Motors Ltd. in 1964, the American corporation was involved with the British Government. This did not change when Peugeot-Citroen acquired Chrysler's European operations. The amount of Parliamentary time consumed by the affairs of both these multinationals has ensured that Linwood has never been far from the public eye.

In the light of these facts the purpose of this chapter is to consider some of the lessons for Scotland emerging from the Chrysler/Peugeot-Citroen case. What should be stressed is that while a number of these certainly relate to the multinational dimension, others concern more general issues of regional and industrial policy in the UK. The story is now complete. The saga which would have required either the restoration of the operation to viability or closure, ended in May 1981 when the Linwood plant was shut. With hindsight this was as inevitable as it was depressing.

123

The Linwood Story[2]

In considering the history of Chrysler and Peugeot-Citroen in Scotland, it is possible to distinguish a number of periods in the years from 1963 to 1981, all of which, while distinct, share the common theme of "hopes raised and hopes dashed".

Period I: Establishment—Amidst great enthusiasm on October 1st, 1960, Lord Rootes announced plans for the Linwood factory. For the Rootes company the plant represented a £23¼m. gamble, to take the manufacturer into the volume car business. The car itself was completely new and commensurately risky, and was to be sold in competition with the Mini which had a strongly established market position. The plant was established on a greenfield site directly across the road from the Pressed Steel Fisher factory, which extended its pressings to supply the necessary car bodies. To meet the needs of the factory, nearly 2000 new homes were built in the village of Linwood and road and rail links and shopping facilities were all improved. Aside from the economic advantages which were expected from the plant, the local M.P. Norman Buchan also saw social benefits, arguing that the project would "contribute to curing the cancer of Glasgow housing."[3]

The Rootes move to Scotland was part of the dispersal of the motor industry undertaken by the Government as part of its more active regional policy in the early 1960s. By refusing industrial development certificates (IDC's) for proposed expansions in existing locations, mainly in the West Midlands, the motor manufacturers were steered towards the North and West. Ford and Vauxhall, however, located their new plants on Merseyside, fairly close to their existing operations; and only Rootes was persuaded to move to Scotland, 250 miles north of their other car production facilities at Ryton (assembly) and Stoke (engines) and the administrative offices and technical centre at Whitley (also in Coventry).

In retrospect the theory underlying the dispersal of the motor industry has proved to be incorrect. The view was that the motor industry, as a location leader, would attract supporting investment in ancillary and components industries. In Scotland, at least, this never occurred and the green fields surrounding the Linwood plant bear witness to the failure of the concept. In this has lain one of the principal problems facing all owners—British, American and French—of the Linwood facility. The cross-hauling of bodies, components and completed vehicles has added to production costs at Linwood. This was particularly significant since the main operations which were undertaken at Linwood were those which were transport cost sensitive, viz. the stamping of body shells (after Chrysler acquired the Pressed Steel Fisher plant in 1966) and the assembly of complete vehicles.

The early euphoria over the Linwood plant evaporated soon after the commencement of manufacture in 1963. In February 1965, the Glasgow Herald was calling the Linwood factory a "running sore", as plant operations were disrupted by constant labour disputes. It was in these very early years that Linwood's strife-ridden reputation was forged. But even now it is difficult to be certain of the true reasons for the labour problems. Among the various factors which have been cited are: inexperience on the part of middle management and the trades unions; the background of the labour force, many of whom came from the traditionally militant ship-building and coal-mining industries; the very different production techniques in the motor industry as compared with those in more traditional sectors; and failure to make adequate provision for the necessary large-scale retraining and re-orientation of workers' attitudes. On top of such issues, which related primarily to the newness of the facility, Rootes were experiencing other problems linked to the failure of the Imp to sell in planned volumes. While this may itself be attributed in part to the inexperienced labour force and other start-up problems, the basic difficulties derived from fundamental design faults in the car. In the first full year of operation (1964), Linwood was operating at only one third of capacity, and a four day week was introduced at the factory in August of that year. Such uncertainties, after the initial high hopes, were hardly conducive to good industrial relations.

Period II: A New Beginning, The Chrysler Takeover—The events at Linwood had an important bearing on Chrysler's entry to the UK market, for it was the deteriorating financial position of Rootes, accentuated by the failure of the Imp, which virtually forced the British company to link up with the American motor firm.

Chrysler Corporation in the early 1960s had no overseas car manufacturing capacity. When Chrysler acquired Dodge in 1929 it took over the small-scale activities of Dodge trucks in the UK. But this was the sole foreign presence until the corporation purchased 15 per cent of the shares of the French company Simca in 1958. Even then, major developments did not really commence until 1963, by which time corporate profitability in the U.S. (a key factor throughout the period Chrysler was involved in Europe) was improving and Chrysler had a new Chairman whose declared aim was major expansion into Europe. The acquisition route was chosen, partly because the costs of establishing a new plant and facilities were prohibitive and partly because of the company's late entry to the European market. In the space of four years, Chrysler entered Europe and took majority or complete ownership of three separate firms: Simca, Barreiros in Spain and Rootes in the UK.

Chrysler's purchase of 30 per cent of the voting shares in Rootes in June 1964 came only after a number of other efforts to establish a manufacturing foothold in the UK had been rebuffed, including approaches to Standard and Leyland Motors. Rootes was neither the first approach nor the first choice. The Rootes-Chrysler arrangement aroused mixed emotions within the country and in Parliament. Since exchange control consent was required the Government was a party to the deal, and under pressure from the Opposition, the Conservative Government insisted that Chrysler should not increase its holdings in Rootes without first consulting the Government. The financial situation of Rootes continued to deteriorate after 1964, with losses rising from £2.1m. in 1965 to £2.6m. in 1966 and £10.5m. in 1967; the loss for Linwood alone in the latter year amounted to £4.5m. The then Labour Government sought a 'national solution' for Rootes by bringing the company into partnership with an indigenous motor manufacturer. This idea was later rejected by Technology Minister Wedgewood Benn because the Government "did not believe that Rootes, by itself, was a viable organisation with or without Government money, owned or not by a British company".[4] Chrysler, understandably anxious to introduce its own management and ideas, was, therefore, permitted to increase its voting interest in Rootes to 66 per cent.

As part of the 1967 takeover, Chrysler agreed to a number of conditions which were made public. Some of these "undertakings" were fairly innocuous and were mere window-dressing, referring to the expansion of employment and exports and the maintenance of a "British interest" in the company. The main political element in the package was the agreement to focus expansion on Linwood: "Chrysler confirms the plans of expansion covering development work at various factories and especially at Linwood in Scotland where the major development will take place and where it is planned to increase employment by several thousands. . ."[5] It is perhaps at this point that the multinational dimension of the Chrysler case first emerges. Chrysler were in a strong bargaining position. Linwood was already showing itself to be the albatross around the neck of the U.K. operations. And yet Chrysler undertook to centre expansion there. The only interpretation is that Chrysler saw in Linwood an even more important bargaining card for the future.

Following the takeover, Chrysler took active steps to try to stem the decline in the British company. A major capital investment programme was instituted, directed towards rationalisation, in-sourcing, facility updating and volume. To increase the capacity utilisation of Linwood, the Scottish operations took over body production which had been previously undertaken by Pressed Steel Fisher Ltd. at Cowley. Linwood thus became the source of body shells for all of Chrysler UK. Assembly of the Arrow range (principally the Hillman Hunter and variants) was shifted to Linwood from late 1969; and with the launch of the Avenger, Linwood benefitted to the extent that the transmission, rear axle and front suspension were scheduled for manufacture in Scotland. From being the Imp plant, Linwood was developed into an integrated facility with a complex product mix covering the entire Chrysler UK range.

The Linwood Experience

Yet profitablity for Chrysler UK (see Appendix 1), and particularly for Linwood, proved elusive for a variety of interrelated reasons. First, the investment programme upon which the company embarked laid too much emphasis in the early years on the improvement of plant facilities to the detriment of investment in new models. The only new car to be built by Chrysler in Britain between 1967 and 1976 was the Avenger, launched in 1970 from Ryton. A number of other models were introduced in Europe as a whole during this period of time. With both the Chrysler 180 and the Chrysler Alpine the declared intention was to launch these models from the UK. But early in 1970 the decision was taken to transfer manufacture of the 180 to France, and again in 1974 the output of the Alpine was switched to France. Production switching, of course, requires multinationalism.

The overt reason in both of these latter instances was industrial relations problems in Britain. Thus a second major reason for Chrysler's failure was that it failed manifestly to handle labour relations in the U.K. Apart from the short unofficial disputes which plagued the British motor industry as a whole, Chrysler was beset by a variety of incidents which led to lengthy stoppages. At Linwood, the first of these occurred in 1968 as the company tried to improve production and eliminate differences in grade structures and payments methods between the original Linwood plant and the pressings facility nearby. Having the agreement of the two major unions but frustrated by smaller unions, the company simply tried to implement its plan. This exacerbated the dispute and eventually a court of enquiry was set up, headed by D.J. Robertson. Three major points made by Robertson are worthy of note since they epitomise the labour relations of Chrysler at Linwood:

1. "We conclude that in terms of payment and related benefits this is an Agreement which reasonable men should be able to accept without difficulty."

2. But "urgent attention should now be given to creating adequate machinery for negotiation and consultation".

3. And the company was criticised for implementing an agreement when only the two larger unions had signed it. It was concluded that Chrysler "acted with rapidity in a situation requiring patience".[6]

These same three points emerge time and again in the history of Chrysler's labour relations. The company attempted to introduce far-reaching, well-meaning and innovative changes in labour relations practices, which were undoubtedly in the interests of the UK operation. But procedures were inadequate and the company seemed often to overreact in its handling of disputes. Attempts to end disputes were frequently accompanied by threats to redirect investment in the UK, to switch investment to other European locations or, indeed, to withdraw entirely. As an American-based corporation, Chrysler failed to understand labour-relations in the British motor industry. Some of their problems emerged from the employment of middle and senior managers more in line with practices in the United States than in Europe. The situation may also have been worsened by the intervention of Detroit but there is little evidence on this. On the other hand, union officials at Linwood have frequently complained about the inability of local management to make decisions without higher-level approval.

The worst year for stoppages at Linwood (in terms of manhours lost from internal disputes) was 1973:

	Under 4 hours	Under 1 shift	Under 1 week	Over 1 week	Total	% of Chrysler U.K. Total
Number of disputes by duration at Linwood	261	48	15	0	324	54%

	Internal factors	External factors	Total	% of Chrysler U.K. Total
Manhours (000) lost due to:	731	110	841	26%

Source: S. Young & N. Hood, *Chrysler UK: A Corporation in Transition,* New York: Praeger, 1977, p. 243.

The prevalence of very short stoppages is very evident, and throughout the years Linwood accounted for about 60 per cent of stoppages lasting less than four hours. In 1973, as in other years, the stoppages tended to occur at particularly unfortunate periods such as when the market was booming or when the company was running losses for other reasons.

A third major factor in the 1970s was shortage of finance both at subsidiary and corporate levels. Chrysler's financial policy for its European subsidiaries (individually) was that of self-sustenance. Investment in new models and in plant and equipment was thus dependent upon profitablity. Such a requirement produced a "Catch 22" situation for the British affiliate: unable to make profits for lack of new models, and unable to finance new models because of lack of profits. Even if the corporation wished to help (which it undoubtedly did not), it was unable to assist financially because of its own weak position in the USA.

Ironically, the year (1973) in which which the company made record and almost acceptable profits was the same year in which the fate of Chrysler UK was effectively sealed. The optimism built up by the reorganisation and re-equipment programme and the launch of the Avenger in 1970 had evaporated. The decision taken in June 1973 to halt investment because of labour disputes and the onset of the oil crisis late in the same year sounded the death knell for the U.S. subsidiary.

128

The Linwood Experience

Period III: The 1975/76 Rescue, Another New Beginning—Speculation about the future of Linwood and the other operations of Chrysler UK began to mount in the press during 1974 and adversely affected company sales. UK banks started to refuse to renew short term loans or require Chrysler Corporation guarantees. In spite of huge losses in the US, the American parent was forced to pump $38 million into the British operation between December 1973 and February 1976. An application to Finance for Industry for cash to reschedule loans proved unsuccessful. Finally, and dramatically, on November 3rd, 1975, "the Government (were) presented with a pistol to their head. . . "⁷ as the Chrysler Corporation Chairman outlined three possibilities to the UK Prime Minister: a) liquidation of Chrysler UK as of the end of November 1975; b) Chrysler would give the UK company to the Government; or c) Chrysler would transfer a majority interest to the Government. The first inkling of forthcoming events had come only five days previously when, at a press conference in Detroit, the Chairman and President of Chrysler had made fairly explicit suggestions regarding the disposal of the British operations.⁸ This was multinational imperialism pure and simple.

Given the circumstances, the UK Government was almost bound to have to save Chrysler. Economically, serious effects on the level of employment (estimated at 55,000 directly or indirectly for the UK as a whole) and on the balance of payments, principally due to the loss of an important contract to supply car kits to Iran, were the major factors. Politically, Linwood was the key: the SNP had won 11 seats at the previous general election and were second to Labour in 35 out of its 41 seats. Chrysler was more or less asked to state its terms.

A number of options for saving the UK company were considered. Almost all hinged around the retention of Linwood, in some way. Agreement was reached initially on a deal which involved the closure of Ryton, but the rentention of the Stoke engine plant, Linwood and the truck facilities. In a display of magnaminity Chrysler Corporation proposed that production of the Alpine should be transferred from France to Ryton, to prevent the closure of the latter. (But the reality of the situation was that Chrysler were short of capacity in France.) Under the terms of the deal, the UK Government committed itself to supporting Chrysler UK up to a maximum of £162.5m. between 1976 and 1979, in comparison with a potential corporation commitment of £64m. These sums of money were to cover possible losses and to finance specific capital projects, principally five 'new' or improved models (for details, see Appendix 2).

Linwood was to become the heart of Chrysler UK under the new arrangements: production of an improved Avenger was to be undertaken at Linwood; a new small car, the Chrysler Sunbeam, was to be launched from Linwood in 1977; and a new light car was to be manufactured and launched from Scotland in 1979. While some job losses were to occur at Linwood, they were to be far fewer than at other locations in Britain.

The Corporation's agreement with the Government expressed laudable sentiments regarding integration: "product and model ranges will be planned as an integral part of Chrysler's overall worldwide product plan so that CUK's (Chrysler UK) products will be complementary to, and have a specific and definable position within, the total Chrysler worldwide product offering."[9] Transfer prices were to be determined on an "arms-length" basis. The Government had the right to appoint two directors to the Board of Chrysler UK and required the company to provide quarterly management accounts and other financial information for use by government departments in monitoring. Finally, the company agreed to negotiate a planning agreement with the Government and the unions (Chrysler, as it turned out was the sole private firm to sign a planning agreement before the fall of the Labour Government in 1979). All of this, of course, smacked suspiciously of some of the commitments made by Chrysler in 1967 at the time of takeover.

Virtually all authoritative opinion was of the view that the government rescue of Chrysler UK would not enable the company to attain long-term viability. And in the context of later events, Chrysler's agreement to continue in Britain may be seen as a cynical attempt to improve the saleability of the UK affiliate. But, ostensibly, at least, Chrysler took their commitments seriously and embarked upon a large-scale restructuring and reorganisation programme in 1976. The Avenger face-lift was duly implemented out of Linwood, and the Sunbeam (mainly using Avenger and Alpine components) was launched in July 1977. The "Glasgow Herald", which like the rest of the Scottish press has fluctuated between extreme optimism and extreme pessimism over Chrysler, commented that "if it is marketed properly, proves reliable and is available on demand, the new Sunbeam should prove a success and the saviour of Chrysler Scotland and Chrysler UK".[10] There were hopes that the Planning Agreement would usher in a new era of harmonious labour relations. On the other hand an unofficial 12 day strike by 450 men in K block (so-called "Crazy-K") in March 1977 over an apparently trivial issue suggested that little had been learned over ten years.

Period IV: The End of Chrysler, Enter Peugeot-Citroen—It was obvious that it would be no easy task to create a viable Chrysler operation in the United Kingdom. The company recorded losses of £42.6m. in 1976 and £21.5m. in 1977. These were covered by the terms of the rescue agreement with the Government, but into 1978 the need to earn profits began to be of crucial importance. Without profitability there could be no hope of financing new model development after the rescue agreement expired. A small profit in the first quarter of 1978, as the Sunbeam established itself, gave promise

The Linwood Experience

of brighter things. But in the second quarter Chrysler UK plunged back into
the red, primarily because of a sharp increase in disputes at some of the
English factories. A major dispute then erupted at Linwood late in June
1978, which, while directly involving only 550 paintshop workers, led to the
laying off of a further 5000 of the plant's 9500 employees. For the whole
year losses amounted to another horrific £20m.

Speculation over Linwood's future began to mount again. In France,
Chrysler launched a new car, the Horizon, which in appearance was very
similar to the Sunbeam. While selling at a similar price to the latter, it was a
front wheel drive car (against the Sunbeam's conventional drive), and it had
five doors (against the Sunbeam's three) and generally was more sophisticated. The Sunbeam was a car for the UK market, given the Continental
European preference for front wheel drive, but it was also faced with competition from the Horizon on the British market. The futility of a rescue
programme for Chrysler UK in isolation was very apparent: Chrysler's long-
term planning clearly did not foresee any integration between its various
European subsidiaries. By leaving the UK operation as a separate entity, the
option always existed of selling it or liquidating it without affecting the rest of
the European facilities. The second factor leading to renewed fears for the
future of Linwood was the decision taken to transfer production of a new light
car from Scotland to Ryton. As the rescue agreement indicated, this car was
to be launched from Linwood in 1979. Finally, there were rumours that
Chrysler were having talks with Mitsubishi Motor Corporation about the
possibility of the Japanese firm moving into Linwood to make cars.[11]

What actually occurred was, again, completely unexpected. Early in August
1978 it was announced that Peugeot-Citroen would take over Chrysler's entire
European car and truck operations in return for $230m. cash and 15 per cent of the
shares in the enlarged French company. Just as the withdrawal ultimatum revealed
the unacceptable face of multinationalism, so also did Chrysler's sell-out. The U.K.
Government was given no prior warning of the proposed deal. This was in spite of
Government financial support and in spite of the corporation's commitment
to a planning agreement. The latter was specifically designed to involve
union and Government in any discussions which took place about the future
of the UK affiliate.

The British Government had little leverage in its subsequent discussions
with Peugeot-Citroen. Doubtless the French giant (now the largest manufacturer in Europe) would have preferred to leave Chrysler UK out of the deal.
In essence, therefore, the Declaration of Intent between Chrysler and the
British Government passed to Peugeot-Citroen. The commitment to the
maintenance of employment made in the existing Declaration was, however,
weakened with the addition of the phrase "to the extent consistent with
prevailing economic conditions". The government agreed to continue its
support programme for the British company and the loan guarantees passed
intact to the new parent corporation. The planning agreement was also to

131

continue. The one addition in the Declaration was the agreement to allow British component suppliers to compete for business within the Peugeot-Citroen group as a whole.[12]

Complete control did not pass to the French multinational until 31st October 1980, but in July 1979 the name of Chrysler Europe was changed to Talbot as the French combine began the enormous task of restructuring. The motive for the acquisition of the U.K. arm of Chrysler Europe was seen by many as being access to the dealer network in Britain. Ostensibly at least, however, Peugeot S.A. set about trying to create a viable Talbot production operation in the U.K. Environmental factors were hardly helpful to these efforts: political turmoil in Iran led to the suspension of the major contract to supply car kits; continuing recession conditions led to a further diminution of the size of the UK car market, and the growth of Japanese imports reduced the market share available to domestic suppliers. On top of this, the launch of the Solara, a saloon car version of the Alpine, from Ryton in 1980 proved singularly unsuccessful.

Linwood had no new models and this time no political saviour. In the face of massive losses for the Peugeot-Citroen group as a whole, the closure of the Scottish factory took place on May 22nd 1981. The UK Government's attempts to save the plant were half-hearted. Cynically the 4,700 Linwood workers added only imperceptibly to the 2½ million already unemployed in the UK. Even among the workers there seemed to be a feeling of inevitability—that time had ultimately run out. To the dismay of the Scottish TUC, the Linwood workforce, by a 2-1 majority, rejected their shop stewards' advice to fight the closure. A chapter in Scottish industrial history had ended.

Lessons for Scotland

This résumé of the history of Chrysler and Peugeot-Citroen in Scotland has tried to point out some of the traumas which have been experienced over the fifteen or so years since multinational companies have had some control at Linwood. It would be wrong to try to generalise these experiences to all multi-national companies (MNC's). Even so, there are a number of important lessons which may be drawn from the operation of first, the American and then the French multinational concern:

1. Government and the Promotion of European Integration

Undoubtedly the most important lesson is related to the question of Government involvement with MNC's. Successive governments have patently failed to secure a viable future for Chrysler Scotland. Clearly as the discussion has revealed, there are operational issues over which Governments have little or no influence. Arguably, problems of labour relations and productivity fall into this category (but see 2 below). The more fundamental reason is lack of understanding of the operation of multinational enterprises. Consistently, negotiations undertaken between the British government and the two multinationals have focussed on the viability of the UK company as a separate entity. The focus of negotiations should at least have been Europe-wide in their dimension.

In 1967, when Chrysler took a majority stake in the British company, Ford introduced their 'Ford of Europe' concept. The rationale underlying this was that to obtain maximum benefit from the size of the European market, integration of country subsidiaries was necessary. Only in this way could the economies of scale in the production and marketing of motor vehicles be fully exploited. Of course, it took Ford ten years before the results of their European integration programme bore full fruit in the form of the Fiesta, with its engine blocks from Dagenham, transmissions and axles from Bordeaux, carburettors from Northern Ireland and engine machinery from Valencia in Spain. Chrysler Corporation policy should, from the beginning, have involved the development of an integrated car and commercial vehicle facility for the whole of Europe. This would have required the manufacture of a European product range, with components production and assembly centralised so as to maximise output at any one location. Together with this, a European marketing and distribution network should have been a major priority. Within such a system Linwood would have had a clearly defined European role. Given its peripheral location, this role would probably have been specified in terms of component manufacture.

Instead of this, Chrysler pursued a strategy for its European subsidiaries which stressed the independence of national units and the self-sustenance of these units. Even after the Government rescue this same policy was still being pursued, witness the Horizon and the Sunbeam. It is arguable that given the precarious financial position of Chrysler in the USA, this was the only possible strategy. Chrysler may have hoped that with the restoration of its European affiliates to profitability, the funds made available could be used to finance integration. But if this was the policy, then it was still based on misconceptions viz. that US managerial expertise and experience was the main ingredient required to restore Chrysler UK to profitablity; and that investment in new plant and equipment was more important than investment in new models. For their part, Chrysler argued that the problems in the British affiliate prevented integration. The then Managing Director of Chrysler UK commented that: "The labour-climate, the consistency of supply, whether it be machined parts or built-up cars did give us difficulty in convincing people that we were a good base to be integrated with."[13]

Given the failure of Chrysler to implement an integration strategy, the

British Government's responsibility was clearly to push the company in the direction of greater integration. On successive occasions, however, commitments extracted from the American corporation seemed to presume that Chrysler UK was a national company rather than merely one arm of a multinational. Yet the Government were fully aware, as far back as 1967, that Rootes was too small to survive as an independent unit. To quote Wedgwood-Benn again, "if we had nationalised Rootes we should have been left, even then, with a company which, in technological terms, was not on a scale which could survive at a critical time."[14] During 1975, moreover, the Government had the evidence of three reports on which to draw, all of which emphasised size and scale economies.[15] It would be easy to lay the blame at the door of the short-term and crisis-oriented nature of British Government policy. On top of this, in the case of Chrysler, was a failure to understand multinationalism, multinational strategy and the sources of MNC's bargaining strength.

In regard to this issue of lack of integration, Chrysler is quite atypical in Scotland. The evidence from other US MNC's has shown a clear trend *towards greater integration* as a result of increased competition and heightened cost pressures, technological change, the enlargement of the EEC and the gradual progress being made towards a 'common market'. The objective of Government policy in such cases should be to ensure, as far as possible, that the position of Scottish affiliates is not endangered by the restructuring which is an essential part of integration.

In either event, there is a need to be involved in understanding and monitoring the strategies of MNC's operating in Scotland. In this context, it is worthwhile quoting from the conclusions of a large-scale study of US MNC's in Scotland undertaken by the present authors:[16] "the single most important observation to be made from the study surrounds the need to be closely and continuously involved in monitoring the strategies of corporations in the non-indigenous sector. This is based on several presumptions. Firstly, that these corporations have more locational alternatives open to them than indigenous companies; secondly, that the external locus of decision making will always make it difficult to interpret corporate policies solely through affiliate behaviour; and finally, that clear involvement with the firms is necessary to identify the relationships between the behaviour of individual corporations and their Scottish affiliates. This study has shown, within the limitations of resources and data, that significant trends can be identified by an increased level of involvement with the corporations. *Transition requires continuous monitoring* at both affiliate and corporate level."

2. The Financial Health of Parent MNC's

This issue emerges directly from that above. The past track record and financial health of MNC's requires close and continuing observation both before investment decisions are made in Scotland and subsequently. Chrysler may have been seen by Governments as a desirable parent for the UK operation because it was large and because it was American. Yet its volatile record in the US was evident to even a casual observer. And during the entire period in which Chrysler was operating in Europe, the financial weakness of the corporation in its domestic market had an important bearing on its inability to succeed in Britain. Finance was less of a problem for Peugeot-Citroen initially. Yet in acquiring Chrysler Europe before it had fully assimilated the takeover of Citroen, the French MNC was taking an enormous gamble. In the end, because of continuing recession conditions, the financial resources of Peugeot-Citroen were severely strained.

3. Government and Aid to Multinational Companies

In the light of the comments above, it is clear that it is hardly possible to provide financial assistance to one multinational affiliate and be certain that the affiliate concerned will benefit from the aid. Through manipulative transfer pricing, and the manipulation of intra-firm royalties and licence fees, the financial assistance may be re-directed. Particularly in the case of Chrysler, when the performance of the French subsidiary was so much superior to that of Chrysler UK, events subsequent to the rescue showed that the corporation had no intention of redirecting its investment focus to favour the British company. This is not to say that in different circumstances governments cannot influence the investment strategies of multinational firms. Apart from financial assistance, there are many types of government pressures which may be used to influence corporate decision-making e.g. 'buy-national' policies.

The more important implication of the Chrysler/Peugeot-Citroen case relating to government aid does not apply solely to MNC's. Apart from the strategic reason for failure viz. lack of integration, a further important factor was poor internal performance. Knowing this, it was not sensible to provide aid without strings. A management and workforce which had failed consistently over a long period of time were suddenly expected to work harmoniously, eliminate disputes and raise productivity. This is not to suggest that the Government should have taken on equity interest in the company. But binding commitments should have been required on issues such as manning levels, productivity, continuity of production etc. In any such situation as that of Linwood not only would this make viability more likely, but it would also allow the Government to extricate itself if the agreed levels of output and productivity were not being achieved.

4. The Branch Factory Syndrome

There is evidence from Scotland of many MNC affiliates being operated as branch plants. The firms' presence in Scotland is limited to production units, with in some cases only very low levels of production decision-making responsibility existing at factory level. Other characteristics of branch plants would include absence of R & D (often centralised at the headquarters of the MNC); absence of marketing functions (usually located in the South of England); low expenditure ceiling for local management without authorisation from above; low level of responsibility in personnel decision-making; plants operated as cost rather than as profit centres, etc. The end results of all these factors are that plants are completely dependent on outside decision-making for their existence and expansion. Chrysler at Linwood was a perfect example of such a branch plant, and therein may have lain at least some of its problems, particularly in the area of labour relations. Naturally, if Chrysler had been integrated on a European-wide basis along the lines suggested above, it would not be possible nor would it be desirable to have decentralisation of decision-making in most of the areas noted. Labour relations may be the one exception, where this is better handled in a decentralised manner by management on the spot. Labour relations, too, is perhaps the major area where a 'culture-gap' exists between foreign and British management and where therefore local as opposed to foreign managerial personnel are preferable.

5. Multinationals and Bargaining Strength

MNC's are in a much stronger position than national companies to bargain with groups in host countries, whether these groups be labour unions, suppliers, governments etc. The threats made by multinational owners at various times to curtail investment, switch investment or even to withdraw may have been counter-productive in some instances. In general nevertheless, they are reflections of the strength of MNC's deriving from their size and multinationality. But the negotiating groups also have their own bargaining counters e.g. governments may influence access to the market or may make withdrawal highly expensive through redundancy payments. The important point is that host country groups must carefully identify where their own strengths lie, and where the weaknesses of the multinational lie. This, in turn, requires information and relates back to other issues of monitoring.

6. Regional Policy

The other lessons from the Linwood experience relate to regional and industrial policy. With the benefit of hindsight, it was clearly a mistake to locate a new factory with a new labour-force and building a new car at Linwood. There were too many imponderables and possibilities for error in this situation. A smaller-scale, less ambitious venture would clearly have been preferable. Given the nature of technological change, however, there is less likelihood of massive projects of this nature in the future, whether from national or multinational sources. The other misjudgement in the case of

Linwood concerned its potential for attracting ancillary industry. This was a major gamble which failed.

Reviewing the case overall, one is struck by the comment of *The Times*, as long ago as 1969, when it remarked pessimistically that: "The outcome (of Linwood) . . . points to the conclusion that the experiment ought never to be repeated."[17]

Appendix 1
Selected Figures for Chrysler UK & Talbot UK

	1967	1968	1969	1970	1971	1972	1973	1974	1975	1976	1977	1978	1979
Chrysler UK (a) **Talbot UK**													
Output (000 units) (b)	210	214	245	249	308	288	292	287	246	159	185	214	121
Employment (000)	na	24.3	25.4	27.7	28.5	25.8	30.9	31.0	28.4	20.6	22.8	25.2	23.9
Sales (million £)	171	176	165	179	320	281	322	313	351	332	458	610	575
Net Earnings (million £) (c)	(10.5)	3.1	0.6	(10.9	0.5	1.6	3.8	(17.7)	(35.5)	(1.4)	(11.5)	(5.2)	(31.1)
Chrysler Scotland/ **Tablot Scotland (Linwood)**													
Output (000 units)	47	44	33	125	127	145	143	157	154	40(d)	60	98	71
of which:													
Built-up (000 units)	45	43	31	68	76	88	81	72	35	na	na	na	na
Knock-down (000 units) (e)	2	1	1	57	51	57	62	85	119	na	na	na	na

Notes:
(a) In 1971, financial period was 16 months to end November. In 1973 financial period was 13 months to end December.
(b) Cars and commercial vehicles. Calender year data.
(c) Bracketed figures indicate losses.
(d) Partly estimated.
(e) Knock-down units mainly consisted of supply of Hunters to Iran.

Sources: Young & Hood, Chrysler UK, op. cit, p. 271; S. Young & N. Hood, "Multinational and Host Governments: Lessons from the Case of Chrysler UK", **Columbia Journal of World Business**, Summer 1977; company accounts.

138

Appendix 2

Financial Arrangements Agreed Between the U.K. Government and Chrysler Corporation

Potential Government Commitment

£50 million maximum share of loss in 1976   )
£10 million maximum share of loss in 1977   ) Funding of possible losses
                                                     (a)

£12.5 million maximum share of loss in 1978 & 1979

£28 million loan for capital development in 1976-77   )
   (guaranteed by Chrysler Corporation) (b)   )
) Loans to finance
£27 million loan for capital development in 1978-79   ) specific capital
   (secured on Chrysler U.K.) (b)   ) projects.
)
£35 million medium-term bank loan facilities   )
   guaranteed by government (and counterguaranteed   )
   by Chrysler Corporation)   )
£162.5 million

Potential Chrysler Corporation Commitment
£10 million maximum share of loss in 1976   )
£10 million maximum share of loss in 1977   ) Funding of possible
) losses(a)
£12.5 million maximum share of loss in 1978 & 1979   )

£10-12 million for the C6 (Alpine) model introduction

£19..72 million waiver of loans (and interest) made to Chrysler U.K.

Notes: (a)   Government responsible for first £40 million of losses in 1976. Equal sharing of further losses in 1976 and possible losses in 1976 and possible losses in 1977-79 up to maximum figures shown.

              (b)   Government loans repayable in ten semi-annual instalments between 1985 and 1990.

Source: Young & Hood, *Chrysler U.K.*, op.cit, pp. 315-7.

References

1. For data on U.S. MNE's in Scotland, see N. Hood & S. Young, *European Development Strategies of US-Owned Manufacturing Companies Located in Scotland,* Edinburgh: HMSO, 1980.

2. For full details and an assessment of the Chrysler case consult S. Young & N. Hood, *Chrysler UK: A Corporation in Transition,* New York: Praeger, 1977.

3. N. Buchan, "Linwood Story", *New Statesman,* 4th December 1964.

4. Cited in Young & Hood, *Chrysler UK,* op.cit., p.83.

5. Ibid, p.102.

6. *Report of the Court of Inquiry under Professor D.J. Robertson into a dispute at Rootes Motors Ltd., Linwood,* Cmnd 3692, London: July 1968.

7. Cited in Young & Hood, *Chrysler UK,* op.cit., p.282.

8. Ibid, p.281.

9. Ibid, p.315.

10. "Sunbeam is Linwood's Ray of Hope", *Glasgow Herald,* 18th July 1977.

11. "Chrysler Pressed to Sell Linwood Plant to Japanese", *Sunday Times,* 2nd July 1979.

12. For further details see *The Economist,* 12th August 1978, p.69 and 30th September 1978, p. 102.

13. Don Lander in evidence to the Expenditure Committee. Eighth Report from the Expenditure Committee, *Public Expenditure on Chrysler UK Ltd,* HC 596(I), Session 1975-76, London: HMSO, 1976, Para. 231.

14. Young & Hood, *Chrysler UK,* op.cit., p.83.

15. In time sequence, the three were: *British Leyland: The Next Decade,* HC 342, London: HMSO, April 1974; Fourteenth Report from the Expenditure Committee, *The Motor Vehicle Industry,* HC 617, Session 1974-75, London: HMSO, August 1975; Central Policy Review Staff, *The Future of the British Car Industry,* London: HMSO, 1975.

16. Hood & Young, *European Development Strategies of US-Owned Manufacturing Companies,* op.cit.

17. *The Times,* London, 23rd May 1969.

THE CROMARTY FIRTH

by George Rosie

To some extent, what has happened in and around the Cromarty Firth in the last ten years or so is a handy metaphor for what has been happening in Scotland. Like Scotland as a whole, the Cromarty Firth was—and remains—a depressed region with a run-down economy, accustomed to dealing from a position of weakness, and desperate to attract cash and jobs. In the early to mid-1970s it was suddenly faced with an invasion of huge, multi-national companies and their associates, all intent on exploiting the natural resources of the North Sea, with the enthusiastic backing of the British Government.

All through the 1970's—and especially in the first half—promises were made, hopes raised, ambitious, grandiose schemes floated. The air was buzzing with the prospect of thousands of jobs, careers, security, affluence, comfort. A better future was on the way. But very little got beyond the dream stage. Most of the big plans and big projects petered out in apathy and hostility, acrimony and disappointment, leaving a local population soured by the experience, and hanging on grimly to the relatively few jobs and developments which actually managed to get off the ground.

In the background—and sometimes very deep in the background—powerful corporations, wealthy individuals, and shrewd locals, have for years been stalking the Cromarty Firth, quietly buying up land, and jockeying for the choice sites, the most likely stretches of foreshore and beach. Not that the land-dealers have been all-seeing and endlessly wise; only the Far Left believes in the omniscience of capitalists. Millions have been squandered, many apparently 'dynamic' and energetic businessmen have had their fingers badly burned and some local farmers have been happily buying back (cheaply) land that they sold for a huge profit only a few years previously.

But the Cromarty Firth has offered an intriguing example of the 'interface' between big industry and local and national politics. The succession of case histories over the past ten years provides a neat demonstration of how multi-national companies—in one case the privately-owned coporation of the richest man on earth—apply their muscle to local, Scottish and British political institutions. And how, in the end, the best sites now belong to a handful of huge foreign companies who (as, when and if the opportunity finally arises) will use them to make fortunes from the North Sea oil and gas.

The money-spinning potential of the Cromarty Firth began to emerge in the late 18th century. The first to take real advantage of the Firth's combination of deep water and strategic situation was a fast-moving, hard-headed young businessman called William Forsyth who had an eye for the main chance and the nerve to stick his money behind his hunches. In 1772 young Forsyth was joined in Cromarty by another well-financed far-seeing entrepreneur, who had even bigger plans for the area. George Ross, a local man who had made a fortune as 'army agent' to the British Army, returned to Cromarty at the age of 71. Between them, Ross and Forsyth transformed Cromarty from a huddle of tide-besieged cottages into a handsome useful 18th century town, with a hard-working harbour and a collection of very decent public buildings.

But while the *town* of Cromarty was thriving, things on the other side of the Cromarty Firth and on the Black Isle were taking a distinct turn for the worse. The local gentry were hell bent on 'improving' their estates, which meant the local population were being replaced by sheep. By the middle of the 19th century the clearing of the straths and glens was almost complete. Thousands of people had been driven to the coast, into the cities of the south, or onto the emigrant ships to the US, Canada and Australia. The only source of capital in the area came from the Royal Navy who were delighted by the Cromarty Firth as a deepwater, sheltered anchorage. The shopkeepers and pub owners of Invergordon did well enough from stranded matelots, but there were very few jobs attached to the RN installations.

However, the sheer potential of the place continued to haunt the plans of many people in the North of Scotland. The Firth had, after all, just the combination of assets that were prized by industrialists elsewhere in Europe; deep water, flat land, good anchorages, a fair-sized population, half-decent roads, a railway, and a well-established 'infrastructure' of schools, houses, communities etc. In the 1960's a powerful pro-industry lobby began to emerge in that corner of Scotland led by people who were dedicated to solving the area's problems by bringing in big companies, big plant, big industry; not, they made it plain, the penny-ante arts and crafts stuff so beloved of planners elsewhere in the Highlands but the real thing— petrochemicals perhaps, oil refining, engineering, fertiliser processing— something big enough to break the vicious spiral of unemployment, low wages, and the southward drift of talented people. They wanted the kind of industry that would generate jobs, skills, careers, money, security, affluence, that would give bright local youngsters a reason to stay in the area, that would spin off in all directions, that would drum up dozens of supply and service industries, professions and consultancies. Something that would put belly, muscle and fire into the economy of northern Scotland.

It was—and remains—a bold and honourable dream. But it is one which has conjured up dour, and often surprisingly effective, opposition from the local landowners, conservationists, and most lethal of all, the well-organised well-educated, well-financed farmers and gentry of Easter Ross. And ironically, one of the most powerful voices in the pro-industry lobby-perhaps the most powerful—belongs to an Easter Ross farmer, John Cameron Robertson of Castlecraig Farm, Nigg. For many years Robertson has worked closely with his friend and business associate Dr Jonathan Mowbray Jenkins, an industrial chemist from the south of England who believes firmly that the Cromarty Firth is probably the best remaining industrial site in Britain. The influence of these two men on the Cromarty Firth area over the past fifteen years or so has been enormous.

Working in tandem, Jenkins and Robertson have either originated or been associated with almost every big industrial project which has been floated for the area. Their activities have won both Jenkins and Robertson local reputations which are remarkable; people in Easter Ross either admire them hugely for their energy and enterprise, or bitterly resent them for much the same qualities. Robertson is a local man, an enterprising dairy and pig farmer, while Jenkins runs a petrochemical consultancy in the south of England from where he maintains a global network of contacts. Robertson is ebullient, outgoing, a forceful talker and debater. Jenkins works quietly in the background, putting together intricate deals, and tightening up the nuts and bolts when they look like loosening. "They're one hell of a team" says a local politician who knows both men well, "and they've been running together for a long time. Jenkins is a pretty inscrutable kind of bloke, doesn't say much, but what he does say is interesting. But John Robertson I know well. And he's the best natural politician I know, a rough man in a debate. He could argue anybody into the ground, and that includes the entire British Cabinet."

When Harold Wilson's government set up the Highlands & Islands Development Board (HIDB) in 1965 to try to inject some life into the ailing economy of northern Scotland, John Robertson was appointed to the Board. He says that he accepted the job on the clear understanding that he was in favour of "big industry, big projects, doing the simple things first and the harder things second, and not going for lame ducks". Jonathan Jenkins was hired by the HIDB as an industrial consultant (at the rate of £40 a day for a minimum of 12 days a month). Robertson says that was when he and Jenkins became firm friends. "I'm a great admirer of his" Robertson says, "Jonathan is an absolutely sterling personal character. . . a super guy."

Robertson claims that he and Jenkins were instrumental in coaxing the American aluminium industry into the Cromarty Firth. "It was in December 1966", he says, "Jonathan and I were in New York. He suddenly said, 'Look, why don't we go and see Nathaniel Davies of ALCAN?' So we pitched up to the ALCAN building and said 'Can we see the President?' They said 'Yes' and we saw him." Robertson claims that because he and Jenkins whetted ALCAN's interest in the site, Reynolds

Industries moved into the game and eventually won the struggle to site an aluminium smelter at Invergordon. (The smelter was eventually built by a Reynold's subsidiary called British Aluminium.) "And that was the genesis of the smelter" Robertson says, although there are a number of people in the Highlands who would dispute his view of the affair.

Robertson and Jenkins were also heavily involved in the attempt to persuade the up and coming independent oil company Occidental, which now has extensive North Sea Oil holdings, to build a petro-chemical and phosphate processing plant on the Cromarty Firth.

Occidental is run by the astonishing Armand Hammer, one of the most intriguing of the oil-industry swashbucklers, an ardent free-enterprise capitalist, who has excellent lines of communication into the Kremlin dating from the time he knew Lenin. He qualified as a medical doctor but made his first fortune shipping goods in and out of the fledgling Soviet Union. He sold priceless works of art in department stores like Gimbels and Saks in New York, made another fortune distilling Kentucky whisky, breeds Aberdeen Angus cattle, and drifted into the oil industry in 1957 when he bought the near-bankrupt California company called Occidental as a tax shelter. At the time Occidental's assets consisted of "nine creaking oil wells producing in total perhaps a hundred barrels a day"; now 'Oxy' is number eleven in the roll-call of oil companies with a reputation as the most restless, thrusting, and energetic of the independents. Robertson, who met Hammer during the negotiations, describes the wily old businessman as "a great old guy".

Robertson is still bitter about the way the Oxy/Hammer project died under a hail of objection and abuse. "I remember Hugh Fraser—Lord Lovat's son—saying there was a vast over-capacity of fertiliser, that it couldn't be sold throughout the world, and that Oxy's phosphates could only compete with the UK. What did we see two years later? Bloody enormous worldwide shortage of fertiliser, prices near quintupled, and huge imports of fertilisers in to the UK." Robertson says it was the intensity and ferocity of the opposition that scared Hammer off. "Oxy said, 'Wait a minute fellows, we don't do dusiness when the bullets are flying. Goodbye chaps!'."

But the Robertson-Jenkins axis was far from defeated. At the beginning of 1968 Jenkins brought in a Scottish businessman called Eoin Mekie, a director of Grampian Shipyards. Jenkins convinced Mekie and his colleagues that there was a big future for petro-chemicals in the Cromarty Firth area, and that same year they formed a company called Grampian Chemicals. Once again Jonathan Jenkins found American finance, this time from Planet Oil of New York who in turn were financed by the Manhattan bankers, Allen Brothers. In September 1968 Jonathan Jenkins joined the board of

Grampian Chemicals, and that year the company began buying up strategically-sited land at Delny and Nigg on the north side of the Cromarty Firth. One slice of land they bought was 220 acres of John Robertson's dairy farm, for which they paid £140,000.

With Jonathan Jenkins on the board of Grampian Chemicals, his friend and ally John Robertson shifted his formidable energies into local politics. In 1970 when Marjory Linklater, widow of the novelist Eric Linklater, retired from Ross & Cromarty County Council John Roberton decided to contest the seat on the rousing platform of: 'The Time for Industry is Now'. His opponent in the election was his own sister, Anne, wife of Robert Hunter Gordon of Pitcalzean Mains Farm. "Interesting elections those", Robertson recalls, "very much a pro-development or anti-development affair. But the antis—the people who wanted to *stop* industry—were very much the upper-middle class, especially the ones who moved into the area after the war. There was a lot of 'for God's sake don't let's make servants too expensive' kind of talk at the time . . . "

The result was hardly in doubt. Robertson defeated his sister easily. He took his seat on the council in May 1970 and before long was Chairman of the Council's Planning & Development Committee and one of the most influential and powerful local politicians north of Inverness.

Although most of the Grampian Chemicals project had received planning permission by 1969/70, by the middle of 1970 things were going badly for the company in other areas. Jonathan Jenkins left the board of the company, and at the end of the year Grampian reported to their parent company, Planet Oil of New York, that they were unable to raise any more cash. According to Dr Tony MacKay of Aberdeen University, Allen Brothers of New York were prepared to stump up a few millions to Planet on the strength of the land they owned but that was all. "Eventually Planet could not name their sources of supply (for crude oil)" MacKay says, "nor could they name the markets for their product, or any details of contracts. So Allen Brothers refused to put up any more money." The Manhattan bankers had decided that Grampian's scheme was a highly speculative venture, without secure sources of supply, contracts, or potential markets. So they pulled the rug out from under Grampian Chemicals.

The collapse of Grampian Chemicals is regarded in the Cromarty Firth area as a 'disaster' or 'fiasco' but John Robertson sees it another way. "OK! So it didn't go ahead" he says. "How perfectly scandalous! But how many other bloody projects didn't go ahead at that time? That was the time Rolls Royce went bust. When Burmah laid the foundations for their collapse. And when the Upper Clyde Shipbuilders disintegrated." Robertson makes the point that all that happened was that Planet Oil (via Grampian Chemicals)

The Cromarty Firth

poured large sums of money into Britain. "Did anybody else lose any money? Answer: no. Was any public investment made and wasted? Answer: no. What was the effect on the balance of payments? Answer: about 5½ million dollars accruing to Britain that wouldn't have accrued if that 'fiasco' hadn't come about. All I can say is we need a regular supply of fiascos like that . . . "

In New York, Planet Oil were in a bind and had to move smartly to avoid disaster. Their corporate vehicle in Scotland was in ruins, and their bankers were putting on the squeeze. The only way out was to do some kind of deal on the site they owned at Nigg Point and at Delny, both now zoned for industrial use and with planning permission attached. Planet Oil took their problem to Daniel K Ludwig, the enigmatic billionaire, and since the death of Howard Hughes, probably the richest man in the world. Ludwig was the sole owner of the National Bulk Carriers group of companies, the biggest privately-owned corporation in the world. Despite his other interests, the 82 year old Ludwig was interested in the Cromarty Firth area. The cash-spinning potential of the North Sea was becoming apparent, and here was a prime site, with industrial zoning, on the edge of a deepwater channel within a few hundred miles of every oilfield in the North Sea. In was an enticing prospect. Ludwig's men opened negotiations with the men from Planet, and made an offer for the land, subject to a six-month delay while they ran a feasibility study.

Planet, however, could not wait. For once Ludwig's operators were beaten to the punch. Also in the running for the land around the Cromarty Firth was a British land-development company called the Cromarty Firth Development Co, one of the three operating arms of the Onshore Investments Ltd (OIL). Although Onshore Investments was registered in Edinburgh, and heavily backed by Edinburgh money, it was owned by the Mount St Bernard Trust, which in turn was owned by Blue Oak Ltd, and the whole string was run by a North of England businessman called John Foulerton. Foulerton's three Scottish companies—the Cromarty Firth Development Company, Peterhead & Fraserburgh Estates, and Nordport—were in a fever of land-buying, and the money was being supplied by Edinburgh investment funds, North Sea Assets and Atlantic Assets. Both these were run by the fund managers Ivory & Sime, the boss of which was the *éminence grise* of Edinburgh financiers, James Gammell.

An executive of the Cromarty Firth Development Co (CFDC) explains the way the deal was struck with Planet Oil. "We put our offer on the table and said 'take it or leave it'. In fact, we put a 24-hour deadline on it. Planet had the option of selling to us for cash, or waiting six months while Ludwig's people did a feasibility study. And even then they might not come back with the right answer."

146

Planet had little choice. In July 1972 they sold their land-holdings to the CFDC in two parcels; 376 acres of flat coastal land at Delny near Invergordon for £490,500 plus another 220 acres at Nigg Point, the same land which John Robertson had sold to Grampian Chemicals in 1968 for £140,000. These two deals gave the CFDC the best industrially-zoned land on the Cromarty Firth as the first deposits in a land bank to which they were to add over the next two years.

The land was no mean asset. In 1972/73 the Cromarty Firth was the centre of a frenzy of activity, as oilfield supply companies scrambled to break into the platform-building industry. Within a couple of years almost every likely site had been snapped up by the big operators. Land which for generations had belonged to local gentry, farmers and distilleries suddenly passed into the hands of international companies based in London, Edinburgh, Italy, Idaho, Houston or New York. The quiet backwater of the Cromarty Firth had moved into the centre of a massive economic and industrial game which was being controlled a long way from Easter Ross or the Black Isle.

The Cromarty Firth Development Company very quickly began to float huge, not to say grandiose, industrial ideas for the area. "The idea was to get British companies behind some of the major industrial projects by getting a foothold on the land" explains an ex-CFDC executive. The land at Delny was to be developed into " . . . a huge 600-acre industrial estate known as Cromarty Firth Midas" according to the publicity material, with a pier . . . "giving access to the deepwater with the construction of docks". The development at Nigg was seen as including " . . . a wide range of activities based on and including oil refining." The old airstrip at Fearn was to be reopened for full-scale commercial flying— " . . . the company plan to change its name to the Cromarty Firth Airport and hope to arrange scheduled services linking with Inverness airport . . . " And much more in the same vein.

"But the Cromarty Firth Development Company were mainly property people" says one ex-employee. "They had no knowledge at all of petro-chemicals." At which point Johnathan Jenkins reappeared. He was hired by the CFDC as a consultant, and Ian Peters, one-time managing director of CFDC said "We kind of acquired Jonathan along with the land." But another ex-CFDC man sees Jenkins in a much more vital role. "It became pretty clear that the major oil companies were not at all keen on having an oil refinery going on that site" he says. "Jenkins was the obvious man to find a prospective user for the site."

But having spent almost £4 million on land around the Cromarty Firth things began to go sour for the CFDC. Their aggressiveness and speed, and the way in which they snapped up hundreds of acres of prime land stirred up a hornet's nest of Scottish MPs who started shouting 'foul' and claiming that a 'Mafia' of Edinburgh money-men were selling Scotland out from under the people's feet. The publicity was bad news to the hyper-respectable Edinburgh money barons, and there was a 'distinct clash of personalities' between John Foulerton, Chairman of the Onshore Investments group of companies, and James Gammell, who controlled the cash. The Edinburgh financiers pulled their money out and left Foulerton's companies—including the CFDC—stranded and gasping.

It was a blow from which the CFDC never fully recovered. "The company were refunded" says one ex-employee, "but it was done on a short-term basis while the projects in which they were involved were long term. It was clear that nothing was going to happen for ten or fifteen years". It was also a time of raging inflation and soaring interest rates, and the collapse of secondary banking in Britain. By the end of 1973 the writing was on the wall for Foulerton's Scottish operation and all their properties and assets were signed over "by bond and floating charge" to the London merchant bankers, William Brandt and Son.

While the CFDC like most other British property development companies was staggering to its knees from lack of cash, Daniel K. Ludwig's tightly-run privately-funded corporation was awash with ready money. Ludwig's men had not forgotten the prime site at Nigg Point for which they had bid and lost. Jonathan Jenkins was approached by one of Ludwig's agents, (probably Ed Loughney, sometime executive vice-president of Gulf Oil) and asked if some kind of deal could be done over the site. Like Planet Oil before them, the CFDC were in no position to say no! Ludwig's aides made them an offer they could not refuse: 236 acres of Nigg Point for £840,388 to be transferred in August 1973 to one of Ludwig's companies, operating at that time as Alphaclass/Investment Developments.

Once again, the key man was Jonathan Jenkins. "He played a very important part" says one ex CFDC man. "He did most of the dealing with Ed Loughney. But John Notter (one of Ludwig's two right hand men) was floating about in the background. Notter was reporting directly to Ludwig. Or so I understand." One large chunk of land which the CFDC had promised to buy was the 600 acre Pitcalzean Mains Farm owned by Robert Hunter Gordon and his wife Anne. On the 17th April 1974 at a solicitor's office in the town of Dingwall the CFDC handed over a cheque for £1,124,400 to Hunter Gordon. That same day in Inverness the same land was sold for the same price to the Cromarty Petroleum Company (CPC), Daniel Ludwig's newly-formed corporate vehicle in Scotland.

At a cost of just under £2 million Ludwig had taken over more than 800 acres of the most strategically sited land on the east coast of Scotland. Dr Jonathan Jenkins—ex Grampian Chemicals, ex CFDC—was taken on by the Cromarty Petroleum Company as Ludwig's 'European agent' and put in charge of the day-to-day running of the company from its modest offices in Soho.

Ludwig's aides were not long in announcing their plans. On Wednesday the 12th December 1973 the Ross & Cromarty County Council revealed that the Cromarty Petroleum Company (CPC) were asking permission 'in principle' to build a huge oil-refinery valued at £180 million at Nigg Point on the Cromarty Firth. It was a vast project, of astronomic cost, consisting of £180 million worth of intricately connected processing plant, control systems, storage tanks, and tanker terminal, all designed to suck in 10 million tons of crude oil from the North Sea and the Persian Gulf every year, crack it down, and disgorge a variety of high-value energy 'products'. There was to be an elabroate processing core, a subterranean network of storage tanks, and a 1,000 foot long tanker jetty sticking out into the Cromarty Firth, big enough to handle Ludwig's fleet of super tankers and bulk carriers.

The Ludwig project dropped like a depth charge into the already troubled waters of the Cromarty Firth area. Almost as soon as the news of the refinery was out, the pro-refinery and anti-refinery battle lines began to form in the towns and villages around the Cromarty Firth. In favour of the Ludwig project were most of the small traders, the shopkeepers, the pub-owners, the service industries, the local trade unions, the Labour Party, the entire workforce of Highlands Fabricators' platform yard at Nigg, the Liberal Party, most members of the Scottish National Party, and (later on at least) Hamish Gray, the area's Conservative MP (and now Minister of State at the Dept. of Energy).

Lined up against the refinery was a smaller, but well-financed and well-organised army of most of the big farmers, the land owning gentry, the businesses who made their living from tourism (hotels, guest houses, arts and crafts, etc), the fishermen, retired people from the South, the handful of youngish, middle-class drop-outs who had moved into the area, and, of course, everybody who lived right up against the project, and who seemed doomed to live in the glare of Daniel Ludwig's flarestacks.

To steer the project through the endless crosscurrents of interest and counterinterest, Ludwig's men hired the services of London PR man Dean Narayn (who handled the operation at national level) and Allan McGuinness (who handled it at Scottish level). On June 24th 1974 the Ludwig project faced its first hurdle, the planning committee of the Ross & Cromarty County Council. And it fell right away. By a vote of eight to seven, the planning committee voted to give the project the thumbs down, despite some strenuous and brilliant advocacy by John Robertson in favour.

But this was merely an opening skirmish. Immediately the pro-refinery forces began to organise petitions of support, bombard their councillors with telegrams and telephone calls, and generally stir things up. "The reaction was incredible" John Robertson recalls. "I've had 120 telephone calls all saying 'My God, we must have this refinery'. No opposition phone calls. 120 to nil." There is no doubt that in the wake of the planning committee decision to turn down the project, a powerful head of political steam built up in the Cromarty Firth, and most of it in favour of Daniel Ludwig's refinery project.

The refinery's most important allies were probably the shop stewards at the Highlands Fabricators' platform yard at Nigg, most of them left-wing. "It was an opportunity to bring another industry into the area" says Tommy Lafferty, then convener of stewards at Nigg and now a full time official with the AUEW. "By mid 1974 we were getting information that the situation was changing drastically. The oil bubble had burst. It was obvious that all the companies were struggling to obtain platform orders. We wanted jobs for the working class people of Easter Ross." Lafferty and his stewards knew that Ludwig had a reputation as a hard-line, even slightly sinister, right-wing figure and weighed that in the balance. "There were a hell of a lot of allegations about the company", he says, "and a lot of people were saying it was not the kind of company that trade unions should have any association with." But Lafferty's colleagues calculated that the advantages outweighed their objections, and voted to pursue the refinery project with all the energy at their disposal.

Startled by the ferocity of the reaction to the planning committee's thumbs down, and impressed by the number of petitions and letters of support for the refinery, the full Council referred the matter back to the planning committee for reconsideration. On Tuesday, July 30th 1974 the planning committee met to reconsider their decision, and voted by 13 votes to 5 to give CPC the go-ahead. "The company were absolutely delighted", says PR man Dean Narayn.

So much for round two! A week after the planning committee did its *volte face* on the refinery issue, an organisation was formed in Dingwall to be known as the Cromarty Refinery Opposition Workers (or CROW) which was led by a highly able and industrious young politician (of SNP sympathies) called Hamish Stuart. By the end of the year CROW had made enough noise and stirred up enough objection to give the Scottish Office pause. On the 21st November 1975 the Secretary of State for Scotland (then Willie Ross) decided that "a public inquiry should be held into the proposal".

The inquiry opened on Thursday the 11th of February 1975 in the faded Victorian ambience of the Dingwall Town Hall, only to be promptly switched to the plusher and less draughty surroundings of the new County

Buildings. The man in charge was George Maycock, the Scottish Office's senior reporter, and an old hand at the inquiry game. His assessor was Dr Robert Johnston, Principal Scientific Officer with the Department of Agriculture and Fisheries for Scotland.

The inquiry into Daniel Ludwig's refinery project was one of the most complex, expensive, intriguing, and longest-running ever heard in Scotland. It ran for ten weeks, cost over £1 million, provided lucrative work for 5 QC's including a later Lord Advocate, 10 juniors, a long string of solicitors, and heard evidence from dozens of expert, and not so expert witnesses. Almost every question conjured up by Ludwig's plan was dragged out into the light of day. Did the UK need Ludwig's refinery? Did *Scotland* need Ludwig's refinery? What would it do to the local economy? Would the schools, hospitals, roads, housing etc round the Cromarty Firth be able to cope? Would there be spills of crude oil? If so, what would happen to the fish in the Cromarty Firth? Or to the huge variety of bird life around the Firth? Would the refinery pollute the air around Nigg? Would it produce dangerous doses of hydrogen disulphide? Would it reek of chemicals? Would it generate endless and intolerable noise?

Then there were questions about Ludwig himself and his companies. Who was he? What were his plans for the North of Scotland? What kind of corporation did he run? Why did he operate his huge fleet of tankers from Liberia? What kind of reputation did he have in US business circles? Did he really want to build a refinery? Was the refinery a screen for some kind of trans-shipment terminal? Did he simply want the planning permissions in order to sell the site at a huge profit? Or to use it as some kind of counter in a complicated global game? Where was he planning to buy his crude oil? And where did he plan to sell his refined product? (These two questions— the ones which scuppered Planet Oil were to plague the company for years to come.)

It took Geroge Maycock until the middle of December 1975 to sort out all the information which had been presented to him, and in the end he came to the conclusion that he could *not* recommend the Ludwig project to HMG. In a 25-page determination Maycock told Ross that Ludwig's people had failed to make out a good enough case for the refinery. He could find no real need for one, given the over capacity elsewhere in the UK. Nor had he been impressed by the CPC's claim that it could carve its own niche in the market: ". . . I think it might be difficult for Cromarty Petroleum Company as an independent refinery to break into and maintain a place in the European market", Maycock wrote, "or to export to the United States of America". Nor did Maycock think much of the company's secretive ways ". . .which scarcely engender confidence in a more favourable view of their potential for refined products".

But in fact, Maycock was wasting time and ink. In 1975 the SNP tide was reaching its peak and the Labour Party in Scotland was under dire threat. "There was no way that Willie Ross could turn down the jobs that the refinery might have brought to the north of Scotland", says one season-ed Scottish politician. "It would have been the depths of political stupidity." So on March 1st 1976 (a year after the inquiry opened) Ross overrode Maycock's advice on the ground that the refinery project ". . . offers advantages to the area which are more substantial than the Reporter envisaged . . . It would be a very serious step to turn down a development of this kind in an area already identified as an area of industrial growth."

But Ludwig's problems were far from over. The last piece in the jigsaw of land Ludwig was building up was 47½ acres of scrub and sand down at the foreshore at Nigg Point. It was not much, but it was vital. It was the point from which the marine terminal would project into the channel, from where the supertankers would unload their crude, and the product ships take off with their naptha, petroleum, butane, etc. Without the foreshore—no tanker jetty. Without the tanker jetty—no terminal. It was *that* crucial to the Ludwig plan.

Unfortunately for the billionaire from New York, the land was owned by one Michael Nightingale, a south of England banker and commodities merchant, who had bought his way into the Cromarty Estates in the mid 1960's. Michael Nightingale is the kind of man who believes firmly that an Englishman's land is his castle, even if it happens to be in Scotland. Jenkins and the CPC had been trying to buy Nightingale's patch of scrub and sand ever since November 1973, and had turned down offers of leases etc, insisting that they must have the right to own the land before they could consider building their tanker terminal. Nightingale was just as adamant in his refusal to sell. Frustrated by Nightingale, the CPC approached the Ross & Cromarty County Council to ask if they would consider slapping a Compulsory Purchase Order on the land so that the refinery project could go ahead. The council said no because "the company failed to explain to us why Nightingale's lease was unacceptable to them", John Robertson explains.

Then Ludwig's aides sprang a surprise. They invoked the Private Legis-lation Procedure (Scotland) Act of 1936, which gives a private company (such as CPC) the right to ask Parliamentary Commissioners for a com-pulsory order. Providing the commissioner's decision is ratified by Parlia-ment the company have the right to acquire the land. This procedure, high-handed and undemocratic though it sounds, was widely used pre-war to ensure that railway, dock, electrification and gas schemes were able to go ahead over the opposition of recalcitrant landowners.

On the 3rd May 1976 the four Parliamentary Commissioners (Lord Elgin and Lord Strathspey, Sir John Gilmour and Hugh McCartney) met in the Advocates Library in Edinburgh to hear why Ludwig thought it essential to have Nightingale's 47½ acres and why Nightingale thought it essential he should not. After listening to the arguments the four parliamentarians *unanimously* agreed that Nightingale should surrender the land for a fair price and the matter was then handed to the House of Commons for ratification. But as soon as the private bill raised its head in Parliament, Nightingale's own MP, Roger Moate, the Tory MP for Faversham, shouted 'object', then trundled round to the Private Bill office to put down a blocking motion, which meant that the matter had to receive a full-scale parliamentary debate.

The debate began on Monday the 2nd August 1976. To some extent it became a re-run of the public inquiry, with the same questions including the veterans—where was Ludwig to get his crude oil? where is he going to sell his refined product?—being asked about the viability of the whole project. In the process, the hostility to Ludwig patched together an unlikely alliance of Kentish Tories (John Wells and Roger Moate) and Labour MP's (Jeff Rooker, Tam Dalyell, Bob Cryer) all supporting Nightingale, while the Government and most of the Scottish MP's were on the side of Ludwig. The talk and delays ran on and on, and by the end of October, with nothing solved, the whole business petered out with acrimony. A few days after, Dean Narayn, Ludwig's PR wrote an (unpublished) letter to the *Sunday Times*, saying the media publicity had ". . . had its inevitable (albeit unfair) effect on the Members of Parliament who might otherwise have at least given the company's side of the case a fair hearing; and the Bill has died."

But Narayn was despairing too soon. The refinery supporters in the Cromarty Firth area cranked up a new campaign, called it the Support the Cromarty Oil Campaign (SCOT), tapped the enormous fund of support among the trade unions, and began to lean heavily on the government and the Highland Regional Council (HRC). The HRC were already exasperated by Nightingale and his blocking of the refinery project, and voted to consider slapping their own compulsory purchase on Nightingale. The hostility to Nightingale was such that he cracked. "The council clearly had the bit between their teeth" he said later, "and there was no question that the climate had changed. One by one the objectors were disappearing. The mass of opinion had changed the other way."

At the end of November Nightingale struck a deal with Ludwig's people. The CPC agreed to pay Nightingale's family trust the sum of £74,000, and also coughed up another £84,000 for a new fund to be called the Cromarty Trust. This money, Nightingale said in his press release "will enable much to be done for the amenities of the town". Nightingale went on to say that he had been stung by the "accusations of greed made against me" and wished to make it clear that "I shall derive no personal benefit from the sale. My principal concern in all the controversy over the refinery has been the well-being and future prosperity of both the town of Cromarty and its people as a thriving community."

While the protracted controversy over Daniel Ludwig's refinery was going on, an event had taken place which was largely overlooked at the time. In July 1975 the jack-up drilling rig Penrod 65, working in shallow water on block 11/30 only 15 miles from the mainland of Scotland struck oil. The group of companies which had 'lucked in' on block 11/30 were led by Mesa Petroleum of Amarillo in Texas, a company founded (and still run) by a 50-year old Texan named Boone Pickens. Pickens celebrated the announcement by calling the oilfield after his wife Beatrice. Although a modest-sized find with an estimated output of 80,000 barrels a day (compared to 400,000 barrels a day for the giant Forties Field) it was handy enough, and good low-sulphur stuff. Ludwig's men were delighted! Here was oil right on their doorstep. If they could pull off a deal with Boone Pickens and the men from Amarillo, then the refinery could get off to a flying start. The awkward questions—such as where the crude oil was coming from—could be laid to rest once and for all.

Unfortunately, Boone Pickens had his *own* ideas about where he wanted the oil to go. For a start he did not want to run a pipeline into the Cromarty Firth. That was too expensive, the Mesa men argued. The stuff could be uplifted to a mooring point, then piped to tankers without coming near the coast of Scotland. Too dangerous, said Scottish fishing interests and the Highland Council, who were anxious to see the oil going into Ludwig's refinery site. Both sides lobbied the Dept. of Energy; Mesa wanting offshore production plans approved, the Council and the fishermen (and the Scottish industrial lobby) demanding that the oil from Beatrice be piped ashore to the Cromarty Firth.

In the end Mesa lost. The Dept of Energy insisted on a pipeline to come in to the nearest practical landfall (i.e. the Cromarty Firth). The Cromarty Petroleum Company immediately began manoeuvering to make sure that any such pipeline would come into their site. But they were alarmed to find that Mesa had been scouting the Cromarty Firth for a site to build their *own* tanker terminal and tank farm. It was becoming quite plain that, for whatever reason, Boone Pickens wanted nothing to do with Daniel Ludwig. Ludwig's PR men began splashing cold water on the Cromarty Firth, and began to sidle up to the conservationists and objectors much to the amusement to many people on the Cromarty Firth.

It didn't work. In May 1978 Mesa Petroleum, the Cromarty Firth Port Authority and Highlands Fabricators Ltd announced plans to build £50 million-worth of tank farm and tanker terminal completely separate from the Ludwig site. It was a stunning setback to the Ludwig project. "Much as I like the Cromarty Petroleum guys at this end" John Robertson said at the time "they've failed to pull off the deal. Mesa should have been very, very easy . . . they failed to pick up the gold nuggets lying at their feet." But why? Why had seasoned hands like Jonathan Jenkins and Ed Loughney blown the negotiations? "Mesa must have been thinking 'Are those guys actually going to build the thing' ", Robertson says. "Could we end up having spent God knows how much on platforms and pipeline, and find ourselves with no terminal?' "

Within weeks of the Mesa announcement, all the work at the refinery was stopped, and at the beginning of July Dickson Mabon, then Minister of State for Energy announced that the oil refinery was "not a runner now", suggesting hopefully that it was "not the end of the story" but the "beginning of a better one". What Mabon was hinting at was revealed at the beginning of September 1978 when Ludwig's men revealed that the oil refinery plan had been scrapped, to be replaced by a bigger, better, more expensive, more complex, longer-term development for petrochemicals on the same site. The whole elaborate package of technologies was to cost £750 million (at 1978 prices), employ hundreds of people, and take gas from the North Sea and fractionate it into propane, butane, aromatics, gas oils etc.

The idea went off like a damp squib. The locals had heard it all before. "Bunch of junk" said one Texas oilman. "Science fiction" said one Nigg welder and another "Shit, here we go again . . .". Meanwhile, Mesa Petroleum sold out their share of the Beatrice oilfield to the British National Oil Corporation (BNOC) and the BNOC have pushed ahead with their pipeline, tanker farm and tanker terminal at Nigg which is expected to come into operation very soon.

For a few months the Cromarty Firth subsided into resentful apathy. But not for long. It soon became known that the British government were planning, or at least hoping to build a huge network of pipelines to pick up the gas that was being flared off from the oilfields, and bring it ashore somewhere in the Scottish mainland. This 'gas gathering line' galvanised the corporations back to life. At the beginning of 1979 Ludwig sold out a majority interest in the Cromarty Petroleum Company to the American petrochemical giant Dow Chemicals, one of the *bêtes noires* of the American left. In the process Dow acquired most of Ludwig's landholdings on the Cromarty Firth, and then announced a plan to build a huge petrochemical works on land to be reclaimed from Nigg Bay. At the same time the British Gas Corporation lodged a planning application for the same site, as did a Scottish-based company called Highland Hydrocarbons, which was very much the product of the Scottish Council (Development & Industry).

It was an extraordinary state of affairs—three companies, with three near-identical projects, all bidding to build them on the same patch of shore which had yet to be reclaimed from the sea. In fact, Dow Chemicals had a distinct edge. At the end of 1979 they had paid—via their newly acquired company the Cromarty Petroleum Company—the handsome sum of £1.4

million to a man called Howard Waterhouse Robinson, the owner (or at lest representative) of a mysterious company which had baffled everybody on the Cromarty Firth known as Garrulus Glandarius Ltd (the Latin tag for the bird Jay).

Robinson acquired his toehold in the Cromarty Firth in 1971 when he purchased the 500-acre water side estate of Lord Elphinstone of Drumkilbo. Working through a Jersey-registered £100 company called Greengate Ltd, Robinson acquired 'All and the Whole of the lands of the Barony of Tarbat' for the modest sum of £80,000. In the seven page document 'disponing' (i.e. selling) Tarbat Estate to Greengate, there is no mention of the foreshore rights, nor is there any mention in any of the previous sales. This is because in Scotland, unless it can be proved otherwise, the land between the high water and low water mark is the property of the Crown, and is administered by the Crown Estate Commissioners in Edinburgh. In fact, in the late 1960's Lord Elphinstone's solicitors claimed the foreshore for the estate "but we received a very dusty answer indeed" they say "so we didn't press the matter any further."

But the new owners did. Howard Robinson put together a case that by ancient 'use and custom' the foreshore in front of Tarbat Estates belonged to the estate, and backed it with affidavits from elderly locals swearing that the estate had always used the foreshore for collecting mussels, driftwood, gravel, etc. In the end the Crown Estate Commissioners decided to accept the argument, and relinquished their claim to the sandbank at Nigg. It was an absolutely crucial decision and gave Howard Robinson and his company the complete rights over hundreds of acres of foreshore running down to the deepwater channel in the Cromarty Firth.

Howard Robinson was not long in further defining his rights to the sandbanks. In May 1975 Greengate sold the estate, together with the foreshore, to a Gibraltar registered company called Quartet Holdings of Gibraltar Heights. The price paid was £50,000 (i.e. £50,000 less than Greengate had paid Lord Elphinstone). But Quartet Holdings were not the proud owners for long. In July 1976 Quartet split off the sandbank section (600 acres in all) and sold it back to another Howard Robinson Company registered in Jersey, called Garrulus Glandarius. Then in 1979 Robinson completed the transaction by again selling the sandbank off to Dow Chemicals for £1.4 million. The original Tarbat estate for which Robinson paid £80,000 in 1971 remains the property of his companies today.

The Garrulus Glandarius deal was a nifty piece of financial footwork which kept the British press guessing from 1976 to 1980. Robinson is a 67-year old Dublin banker, who runs a fringe bank called the 'City of Dublin Bank' with its HQ in Lower Merrion Street, Dublin. Although described in Dublin business circles as a 'colourful character' Robinson is a minor pillar of the Irish establishment; he is past president of the Chartered Accountants of Ireland (1965-1966) a former member of the Academic Council of Dublin University, one-time treasurer of the Irish Red Cross Society, and a leading light in the Church of Ireland's Representative Church Body, which runs the Church's financial and property affairs. Robinson's son Michael is also a director of the City of Dublin Bank, and his third son Nicholas is married to Senator Mary Robinson, one of Ireland's more liberal Labour Party politicians.

The fact that one Robinson company (Garrulus Glandarius) paid the apparently enormous sum of £600,000 for the sandbank to another Robinson Company (Quartet Holdings) does make sense. Although the Inland Revenue might have some difficulty in pinning down the tangle of Irish and offshore companies for Corporation Tax purposes, it would be very hard for Robinson and his associates to avoid paying Development Land Tax at 60%. But according to the Inland Revenue the £600,000 purchase price (plus another £50,000 'threshold' allowance) would be discounted *before* the company began paying DLT. Which means that instead of paying DLT at 60% on £1.4 million (i.e. a tax bill of £840,000) Garrulus Glandarius will be liable for DLT on only £750,000 (i.e. a tax bill of £450,000), which is, of course, a clear saving of almost £400,000.

Meanwhile, the towns and villages around the Cromarty Firth are still waiting to hear whether or not the gas-gathering line will, finally, come ashore at the Cromarty Firth, and whether or not the petrochemical projects being floated by Dow and the others will ever be built. At the moment the tentative plan is to take the line into St. Fergus, north of Peterhead, take off the ethane, then pipe the remaining gases under the Moray Firth to the Cromarty Firth where it would be used as 'feedstock' for the manufacture of petrochemicals. "But dammit man, folk have been talking like this for near 20 years now" says one irate citizen of Alness. "It's been one bloody project after another, one daft scheme after the next. Spiv after spiv. I'm sick of it all. I'll believe it when I see it."

DETAILS OF AUTHORS

Alan Sinclair is a founder of Scottish Education and Action for Development, and holds a degree in Development Economics from St. Andrews University. He has worked in the development education field in Britain for the past five years.

Roger Jeffery is a Lecturer in Sociology at Edinburgh University. He has made a special study of the history of the Glasgow firm James Finlay, and of other British companies involved in the tea trade.

John Firn is a senior officer of the Scottish Development Agency. He is co-author with Michael Lipton of a major study of relations between Britain and India since independence, and has contributed to many publications including "Scotland 1980".

Nigel Howarth is a Lecturer in Economics at Strathclyde University, who is engaged in a special study of the industrial relations policy of multinational companies.

Rhys Jenkins is a Lecturer in the School of Development Studies at the University of East Anglia.

Stephen Young and **Neil Hood** are respectively Lecturer and Professor in Business Economics at Strathclyde University, and are co-authors of a recent major study on the forward investment policies of multinationals in Scotland.

George Rosie is a freelance journalist and author with an established reputation for investigative reporting, particularly in the field of oil-related developments.

Stephen Maxwell has contributed articles to a variety of Scottish publications and was co-editor of "The Nordic Model: Studies in Public Policy Innovation" (Wilton House, 1980). He is an Organiser of Scottish Education and Action for Development.

158